SPIN MAN

SPIN MAN

With

Special Appearances By:

☆ Willard Scott ☆ Ben's Best Kosher Deli

☆ Dick Clark ☆ Kathryn Crosby ☆ Elke Sommer

☆ AT&T ☆ Scott Brayton ☆ Fred Silverman ☆ NBC

☆ Contact Cold Remedy ☆ Mother Teresa ☆ Yoko Ono

☆ Mayor Koch ☆ Dan Dorfman ☆ Kellogg's ☆ Johnny Mercer

☆ Richard Nixon ☆ Mr. T ☆ Stolichnaya (Stoli) Cristall

☆ Drexel Burnham Lambert ☆ Alamo Rent A Car

☆ Rexall Sundown ☆ Irving Fryar ☆ John Gotti

☆ Regis Philbin ☆ Ron Perelman ☆ Pierre Cardin

☆ James Edward Olmos ☆ Morton Downey Jr.

☆ Famous Amos ☆ Henny Youngman

☆ Tibetan Singing Bowls

☆ Muhammad Ali

And Many

More

SPIN MAN

The topsy-turvy
world of public
relations...
a tell-all tale

THOMAS
J. MADDEN

TransMedia
Publishing, Inc.
Boca Raton, FL

Mr. Madden's neckties are from

© 1997 Thomas J. Madden

Published by Transmedia Publishing, Inc.
Boca Raton, Florida

Madden, Thomas J.

Spin man: the topsy-turvy world of public relations... a tell-all tale / Thomas J. Madden. — Boca Raton, Fla. : Transmedia Pub., 1997.

    p.   ill.   cm.
    Includes index.

    ISBN10: 1-890819-00-X
    ISBN13: 978-1-890819-00-2

    1. Publicity. 2. Public relations. 3. Madden, Thomas J. I. Title.

HM263 .M33 1997   97-61336
659—dc21   CIP

Project Coordination by Jenkins Group, Inc.
www.BookPublishing.com

Production editor: Alex Moore
Interior design: Barbara Hodge

13   12   11   10   09 • 6   5   4   3   2

Printed in the United States of America

To Angel, Andrew and Adrienne
and to my guiding light,
my gorgeous partner and wife,
Angela d' Giovinazzo

When one finds a worthy wife
Her value is far beyond pearls
***From the* Book of PRoverbs**

➤⌒

Contents

Preface

Maddens are everywhere. There are 19,957 households bearing the name worldwide. But people are always asking me if I'm related to just one—John Madden. Well, the truth is I am. Very much so. I'm also related to Jake and Sirena Mazzone. They're my grandchildren. And they call me *NoNo*. That's how they pronounce the Italian word for grandfather. To think of myself as a grandfather is a hard pill for a super-active promoter like me to swallow. It's even tougher to answer to a double negative. But I'm getting used to it.

Probably because I came into this world a Caesarian, I begin the Adventures of The Spin Man in the present and work backwards. Then forwards. My feisty Aunt Mac was right. She always accused me of being *ass backwards*. Her famous expression was *back up nine miles!* So let me start out where I am right now at the pinnacle of flackhood. And to show you just how far this flack has flown—thank you very much, Aunt Mac—I'll back up nine miles.

Please also note I'm an only child of a concert violinist who was an only child. So, allow this story to saw where it pleases. Or you could set off an awful tantrum. And that's not the spin I'd like to put on these memoirs.

What Spins Around

What spins around in public relations can spin back in a miraculous way!

After Rexall Sundown, Inc., asked me to look for a charity it might support, I learned the University of Miami/Jackson Memorial Medical Center needed a pediatric bone marrow transplant center. Soon afterward, *The Rexall Sundown Bone Marrow Transplant Center* was born.

Shortly after that, one of the senior executives at Rexall learned his five-year-old son had cancer. The little boy needed a bone marrow transplant. The sooner the better. So the executive took his son down to Jackson Memorial where he underwent a bone marrow transplant.

A while later the boy was released from the hospital bubble room, designed to keep diseases out and healing in. And today he is victorious against cancer.

Acknowledgments

How Do You Spell Madonna? With Two 'Ns'?

This is one of the 70 questions I've asked my wife and partner, Angela, 70 times in writing this book. For without her assistance, I would have forgotten many of the characters and episodes described herein and undoubtedly misspelled many of their names. This book could not have been written without her assistance, nor could I have survived this crazy life of a spin man without her at my side helping. And helping. And helping.

Together we've promoted a slew of clients, often at the same time, which is like keeping a lot of plates spinning in the air.

spin \spin\ *n.* **1.** having English or rotation intended to achieve a desired interpretation of a particular fact or outcome. **2.** a PR person's or Spin Doctor's tools of trade. **3.** that voodoo that you do so well. **Spin** v., **spun**, **spinning**, n.—v.t. **1.** the act of applying spin. *Nothing spins as sexy as a Broadway show* (Tom Madden). Caution Bill O'Reilly viewers: You are about to enter *The Spin Zone*.

1

Everybody Wants Their Name In The Paper ...
Like Tomorrow!

It's still hurricane season late in September 1996, but mercifully near the end of a torturously long, sweltering summer in South Florida. Our office phones are ringing incessantly. Everyone with something to sell today wants their name in the papers or their mug on TV. So they call a public relations firm. And as America's obsession with publicity filters to all strata of our economy, companies big and small are calling. They want media exposure and they want it ASAP. Because advertising is brassy and overpercussive, they prefer it be in a news story. To them, PR is wood-wind perfection. It doesn't appear as self serving. As a result, firms like ours are bursting at the seams with clients yearning for that third-party endorsement, that halo media bestows that wins them instant respect, that recognition that fires up their business. And those precious moments of fame sending their entrepreneurial spirit soaring. Many believe the exposure we generate as news is more credible and convincing. We encourage that feeling because that's what we do.

We get media to write about our clients and their products in news stories and feature articles; publish their photographs; interview and videotape them; put them on talk shows, radio and television programs;

1

bounce them into homes off satellites from live remotes, drop their names and quotes into columns, editorials, items. Profile them. Investigate them. Whatever! Just spell their name right. Yet we toss half the people who call us for publicity back into the sea. We refuse to represent sharks, eels or guppies. Usually our pre-operative probing scares them off. Or I'll quote such an outrageous fee that we'll never hear back from them. Frequently our due-diligence elicits babbling or what a Fed chairman might term *irrational exuberance.* Mostly it's just plain ignorance over what PR can and cannot do to enhance someone's fortunes in business.

One of the callers this day is a male nurse inquiring about public relations services for his boss, a female plastic surgeon. *What could we do for her? How much would it cost? Would we be interested in submitting a proposal?* They're the typical queries PR firms receive today from businesses and professions. So I cast out my standard line of inquiry. *What's her background? What would she like to achieve? What messages would she like sent? To whom? And what distinguishes her and her practice?* Or put another way, what's so damn interesting, appealing or different about this one plastic surgeon when there are columns of them listed in *The Yellow Pages,* especially in a youth-worshipping place like Boca Raton, where rejuvenation is a religion. If I genuinely think we can help someone's business, and they can afford our services, I'll suggest a meeting at which we can discuss the pertinent facts as a first step to 1) determine if public relations is the appropriate marketing tool for accomplishing certain objectives and 2) design a meaningful program—one that at least has a reasonable chance of being successful, since there can be no guarantees that media will be the slightest bit interested. Do you hear that? No guarantees!

Then the nurse mentions something about Dr. Vivian Hernandez that catches my ear. It's that discordant note I've been trained to listen for. That quirk. Or twist. Some resonating thing that makes somebody or something stand out from the pack. Makes them unique. Maybe newsworthy! She's preparing to perform surgery *pro bono* on a young girl to correct a severe case of breast asymmetry, one of the worst she has ever seen. One breast is four times larger than the other. It could be a story, I thought. And if I think I can interest media in it, then it passes my litmus test for accepting a client. I've reached the point in my career when I'm not looking to struggle anymore. I prefer those lay-ups. What pocket billiard players call *ducks*—balls lined up in front of pockets ready to sink in. Plop! Like the time I found a *bitch* for Boomer.

A Spin Down Niagara Falls

It was an easy promotion to pull off and one of the splashiest. I went to Fred Silverman with the idea while he was still at the helm of NBC and I was his first mate, back in 1981. Seinfeld was still a kibitzer in high school. NBC was getting left back in the ratings. We were in third place. And in those days third was an embarrassing last. On the network's program schedule was a warm and fuzzy anthology series about the misadventures of a lovable collie dog named *BOOMER*, only viewership was slipping badly. And the show was in danger of being sent to the dog pound; maybe being put to sleep. So I had this idea to rekindle viewer interest and Fred told me to run it by the producer on the Coast. A.C. Lyles loved it. So I had NBC conduct a nationwide search for a bitch Boomer could marry and take on a fabulous honeymoon to Niagara Falls. It would make a big publicity splash that the show desperately needed. We found the perfect bitch for Boomer to wed and flew the happy couple to Niagara Falls. After being married by a justice of the peace, they went on a traditional honeymoon ride on the *Maid-Of-The-Mist*. The whirlwind honeymoon culminated in a stopover in Manhattan where Boomer and his bride went for a romantic horse and buggy ride in Central Park. The press was unbelievable. Some newspapers like the *New Orleans Times-Picayune* ran it as a banner story across the top of their front page. For several weeks thereafter the ratings picked up. But then like so many marriages today, the romance cooled. TV viewers once again started losing their ardor for Boomer's day job rescuing little boys and siccing bad guys. Boomer's ungrateful bitch ran off with a husky. NBC affiliates and advertisers started barking at Fred to do something. By now I was in the doghouse. And finally NBC was forced to find a new home for Boomer off the airwaves.

But it was a great marriage while it lasted. And for Boomer? Well, at least he got to see Niagara Falls.

Now one of the staples of PR was barking up my tree. Here was someone doing a good deed to tell the world about. Here's a physician about to help a poor girl with a deformity, who otherwise couldn't afford the operation. How novel was this type of surgery? I asked. *It's been done before, but a case this severe I'd have to say is pretty rare.* Sounds like duck soup to me. Media like their stories rare. They don't have to be earthshaking or even shatteringly new, just something most people haven't heard before. And I hadn't heard of this condition. It's like Watergate still peeling into headlines as historians reveal aspects we don't already know about history's most publicized burglary. The surgery sounds interesting. And could be a perfect media hook with which to pull this lone damselfish out of an anonymous yellow sea swarming with fellow plastic surgeons. Could she market the story herself? Hardly. Often the frog doesn't know he's handsome or that his croak is a ballad. And whom would she call? And would anyone call back? So I suggest that Dr. Hernandez and I meet right away. I'm interested in taking her case. We make an appointment to meet at her office. Mentally I'm already scrubbing up. I can sense Dr. Spin wanted in surgery. Already I'm thinking how I might reconstruct and enlarge her image as she reconstructs a pair of irregular breasts.

Ironically, all year long my PR firm has been focused on breasts, only in connection with a more serious health risk women face—breast cancer. We represent Imaging Diagnostic Systems, a small public company listed in the pink sheets. Its CEO, Dr. Richard Grable, and his partner and wife, Linda Grable, are developing a new breast screening modality for early detection of breast cancer. We've generated articles about their work and have booked them on national TV programs, including one of the last *Donahue* shows. It helped their stock rise from pennies to a high of $8 a share. Since we agreed initially to accept the bulk of our fee in stock, it has made our firm a lot of money. When their stock price shot up, so did our monthly fee.

Their system is an entirely new form of mammography that uses computer technology, algorithms and an ultra high-speed laser that circumnavigates the breast. It can detect the tiniest of cysts or tumors without radiation or any discomfort to the patient from having her breasts compressed as they currently have to be for traditional X-ray type mammography. With this safer, painless method, the patient lies face down on a table and her breasts fit through a porthole allowing the laser to circumnavigate them with unprecedented precision. The images produced are so incredibly clear and accurate that the Grables can hardly contain their excitement. I realize it's an overworked word, but IMDS is truly going to *revolutionize* breast cancer screening.

So we pan now to a more aesthetic view of breasts as we prepare to meet Dr. Hernandez, whose appearance turns out to be a pleasant surprise. Particularly when she smiles, the doctor is a remarkably attractive woman with dark hair, brown eyes, perfect teeth, smooth skin and a milky-white complexion most women would die for. She is not only young-looking and beautiful, but bright and articulate. And she has a charming Cuban accent. We hit it off instantly. She asks about my background and I tell her about all of the medical professionals whose reputations we've successfully treated over the years. She asks if we could possibly reduce the fee I had quoted. I tell her that if cost is an important factor, there were less-expensive PR firms I could recommend whom I'm sure would be glad to represent her. That always gets them. Most clients want the best representation they can afford when their reputation is at stake. She agrees to retain us.

We're not on the case a month, when we score our first major hit for our new client. We get her an interview with CBS News. We told a producer there about the surgery to correct the breast asymmetry and she heard the same dissonant note that I had heard. It piqued her interest enough to want to interview Dr. Hernandez and her patient. The first interview would be by phone. The second was to be on camera in the doctor's office. The piece would air on *CBS This Morning* in February. It's an exceptionally windy and overcast November 1996 when I began preparing Dr. Hernandez for the interviews. We had worked out arrangements for CBS to interview both Dr. Hernandez in her office and her 20-year-old patient, Denise, in a private home that we would arrange. It's a sensitive and compelling story. The asymmetry has deeply affected this young girl emotionally. It has devastated her social life. So ashamed of her deformed breasts, she won't even date. She keeps her problem hidden from everyone. Even her parents didn't know about it until she was 19. Dr. Hernandez has agreed to perform the surgery at no charge. The procedure will make the breasts relatively even by surgically reducing one and enlarging the other with saline implants until they both look normal. At first Denise agrees to be interviewed if she can wear a wig and sunglasses, but then drops the requirement for the disguise.

The main problem comes not with the patient or her deformed breasts, but with Dr. Hernandez. She hates to do interviews. She wants to do this CBS interview, but cameras terrify her. Yet she knows there are other females with asymmetry whom she would like to reach out to, for she knows she can cure it in a procedure that takes only about three hours. She performs it in the surgical room of her pink-colored office on Federal Highway in Boca Raton. Dr. Hernandez' problem stems from her feeling that her English is not what she would like it to be. She was born in Cuba, is a graduate of the University of Illinois Medical School and has trained at Manhattan Eye and Ear Hospital. She is married to a psychiatrist. They have a 16-year-old son. One of our publicists, who is exceedingly well endowed, consults Dr. Hernandez about having her own breasts reduced, but Dr. Hernandez talks her out of it. They decide instead on liposuction for her thighs.

So I begin to operate on her camera phobia. I try to get her to smile more and relax with a camera aimed at her lovely, oval face. The process is called desensitization, or inoculation therapy. The theory is that you expose a subject to small doses of the stimuli that causes fear or anxiety, and little by little you get the subject to relax and be friendly in the presence of bright lights, cameras and even tough questions. Then you show your subject on camera what he or she is doing wrong and how much more effective they are when they're relaxed and friendly. It works every time.

We do these simulated interviews where I ask her everything I can think of about breasts, about enlarging them and reducing them. We discuss all sizes and shapes of breasts and she illustrates by showing me photographs of breasts of women discretely anonymous. And points things out to me about breasts. How they should look. How supple they should be. And about nipples. And I drive back to my office thinking about them. Some of the largest pairs I've ever seen. Deformed? Hardly. Not to me. I find them splendid. Magnificent! And haunting.

A Spin Down Mammary Lane

Now, as early as I can remember, growing up as a flaming heterosexual, I've always been fascinated by that wondrous part of a woman's anatomy. As an adolescent, I perused them by flashlight at night in those magazines boys read under covers and on expeditions into darkest Africa via *National Geographic,* observing tribal women walking naked through jungles with baskets on their head. Later, as an Atlantic City lifeguard, I studied thousands of them bouncing along beaches in bikinis. Still today my eyes follow their shadowy trails down evening gowns at charity balls in the Breakers Hotel of Palm Beach.

Sometimes I catch myself pondering their whereabouts under sweaters or silky chiffon blouses. Now please, I'm not being disrespectful to women, only admiring of that part of them that has stood out in my mind since I was a lad. And I've never referred to the prominent and voluptuous parts as *hooters, honkers* or *Winnebagos.* To the contrary, I'm sensitive to sexual discrimination issues in the workplace, so I avert my gaze from them. I can honestly say at times I forget they're even around during normal business. And these are my symptoms as honestly as I can present them as I work with Dr. Hernandez, one of the world's most beautiful breast surgeons. And we probe one of her specialties: breast reduction and enlargement.

And now you have the background, which explains the dreams I was having of being surrounded by breasts, of feeling pursued like Woody Allen in *Everything You Ever Wanted To Know About Sex.* And I can't sleep some times and flick on the tube. And there's this infomercial late at night for a gel-like breast enhancer called *ACCENTS*. *They're Hollywood's Breast Kept Secret.* And I want to call Dr. Hernandez. Have her prescribe something so I can sleep. But I don't dare do it. Besides, it's almost the weekend. And I'll be able to relax. So by Monday morning I'll be well breasted.

After four sessions, we get her over her camera shyness. Now she's smiling and talking so much on camera I can't shut her up. She even asks for a few extra lessons, I suspect now for the fun of it. When the time for the CBS interview rolls around in December, she is Barbara Walters in a lab coat. Now it's the day before the surgery. CBS interviews Dr. Hernandez in the morning and Denise in the afternoon at a home we provide for maximum privacy. The interview with Dr. Hernandez goes about as well as it can go. She is confidently at ease on camera, articulate and friendly! She talks about the surgery and about the emotional relief she expects Denise will experience afterward—*like a bird released from a cage.* When the hour-long interview is over, Dr. Hernandez asks the producer: *Aren't you going to ask me any more questions?* During the interview with Denise, the producer, the camera crew and Margie, our Executive Vice President, are all in tears recording her touching story. It's heart wrenching, powerful stuff. The next morning, the camera crew shoots parts of the surgery and returns to New York.

Then in January CBS returns for the *after* interviews. For Denise it was as if a miracle had occurred. For the first time in her life she feels normal. An ecstatic feeling of relief sweeps over her from being rid of her deformative burden. Dr. Hernandez expresses pleasure with the results. The piece airs at 8:34 A.M on *CBS This Morning* on February 13, 1997. It is powerful. Brilliantly edited. It's deserving of an award for CBS. For Dr. Hernandez, it's still reverberating in recognition and patients for her thriving practice. Now whenever there's a plastic surgery story, she is a registered source the media call on for comments. So it continues to ripple positive exposure for her. As we knew it would.

Preparing professionals like Dr. Hernandez for media appearances is a specialty of mine. I got into it at American Broadcasting Companies, where I was in charge of three departments, one of which was speech writing. But like most speech writers, you soon discover that writing the speech is only half the process. You have to rehearse executives or they'll screw up the delivery something awful like Fred Silverman did one night in a speech to a group of advertising executives in Chicago.

What'd somebody die in there?, he asks as we leave the hotel after he had delivered my speech. *Yeah Fred, YOU! We should have rehearsed it more.* But I don't dare audiblize the thought.

2

Only In America!

Over the years I've prepped many executives and even doctors, lawyers and Indian chiefs. Well, not quite chiefs, but certainly American Indians, like my dear friend Reuben Silverbird, who is part Navaho, part Apache. We met him when he was singing at La Maganette Restaurant on Manhattan's upper East Side. Reuben called me one day and asked if he could come over. He was trying to come up with a name to call the Native American restaurant that he was planning to open on Columbus Avenue since he had just come into a fortune. He had eloped with Inga, a widow of one of the owners of Chalk Airlines, the small profitable carrier that ferried gamblers between Florida and the Caribbean casinos. Only in America! One day he's singing in the doorway of a restaurant without a pot to tepee in. Now he's downstairs parking his Mercedes. I spot him one cold February morning from our 22nd Street apartment across from the Flat Iron building. He's wearing a fur coat and walking a poodle wearing a fur coat. And on his way up to see me. All I could think of was . . . what a country!

"So what do you think I should call it?"

"Silverbird."

"Yes?"

"Silverbird."

"What?"

"SILVERBIRD!" I shouted. "Call the damn place SILVERBIRD. It's a great name. It's your name. It's Native American. It's sleek. It fits."

A few weeks later Reuben opened the hottest new restaurant in town called Silverbird on trendy Columbus Avenue. They served snake and buffalo meat and banged tom-toms at your table. For the first year, you couldn't get a reservation. Then one day I heard that Reuben banged the wrong tom-toms. Inga vamoosed. The place closed. And Silverbird went down to Disney World, where he got paid to be himself, an American Indian.

. . .

About a year after the massacre at Silverbird's, I was having lunch at the Russian Tea Room with the producer of the then *McNeil Lehrer News Hour* and we talked about having Leonard Goldenson, one of television's pioneers, on the program. I thought it was a great idea. When I presented it to my boss Ellis Moore, he shuddered. *Leonard's never been on that side of the camera in his life*, he explained. *Okay, let's acclimate him like we did Fred*, I said.

I had just finished training ABC Television Network's President Fred Pierce. He had real problems relating to the press. At news conferences, Fred would tighten up at the slightest adversarial question, thrust his square jaw forward, leer at his inquisitor, then lash out in a nasty, arrogant manner. A reporter asked him about his plans to set up a "truth squad" to investigate leaks and sources of unfavorable stories that were surfacing about ABC, sort of like a White House plumbers operation from the earlier Nixon years, and ironically at a time when the network had vaulted to number one in the ratings.

We heard you're going ahead with your truth squad and you hired Sander Vanocur to head it up? Fred would glare at the reporter, chew him up with his piercing eyes, then look down at the floor to where he'd like to spit out his odious question. On a scale of meanness, Fred's answer pushed the needle to irate red. *It's not a truth squad, nor will it be called a truth squad and the implication is entirely erroneous and should be stricken from any future reference!* (Translation: *Fuck You!*) And the more antagonistic Fred became, the meaner the questions got.

It was snowballing into a real PR problem for the company and it had to be fixed. So I rented a television studio on West 57th Street, gathered a group of actors, persuaded Fred to come over and we started simulating news conferences.

At first he treated it like a joke, a sort of game that wasn't going to affect him much. When the lights came on and cameras started recording, however, he stiffened. It was no joke anymore. He was into it. When we fired the questions we knew would annoy him, the face muscles constricted. The jaw turned menacing. Then we'd sit him in front of the VCR and show him how mean he looked. He was amazed. He couldn't believe it.

That's when he decided he needed to improve. We did it again and again, each time suggesting he try different things, like smiling, like walking away from the podium toward his audience like President Clinton would do so effectively a few years later in his second debate with Senator Dole. And soon a metamorphosis began to occur. Fred started to relax. We replaced his dark suits with lighter colors. It seemed to make him warmer, friendlier. After several weeks of training, he was ready for the main event, his next press conference in LA. Minutes before the conference, I gave him a crash refresher course. I had him view a short video tape I had edited of *before* and *after* highlights. Again it made the points. *Be friendly. Relax. Call reporters by their first name. Smile. It's not World War III. Those reporters are just trying to do their job. They're not out to murder you. Use salesmanship. Disarm them. Win them over. Have fun with it Fred. Relax and enjoy the performance. They'll like you.*

The result was nothing short of amazing. He was utterly charming and relaxed in his tan sports jacket. He even joked with the press. When the truth squad question came up this time, Fred smiled. *My reaction, quite candidly, was one of surprise when I first heard the term. There never was any intention to set up anything like that. And the past seven or eight months have demonstrated there is no such thing.* [The needle was moving past *tranquility.*] *Among adult, mature, professional people, we can have honest differences of opinion.* [Now toward *pure love.*] *I think our relationship with the press is a healthy one. And I look forward to it.* Reporters couldn't believe it was the same Fred Pierce. Some even wrote about a distinct change in Fred's demeanor. For a change, the coverage was positive. Even his wife called to thank me. *You know, he's even different at home*, she said.

Bingo! The spin man had spun solid gold. It was a triumph. A PR jackpot. That was no news conference, it was a flat out love affair. Fred fell in love with the press and the press loved him back. What had I created? On the return flight from LA, I drank double scotches and contemplated if I should ask Ellis to double, triple or maybe quadruple my salary.

So I built a set that looked just like the McNeil Lehrer program and we started to desensitize Leonard Goldenson, the man who in the early days of television had persuaded Hollywood not to fear its upstart rival. He told Hollywood that instead of fighting television as a competitor, they should join it. And he brought to ABC the first television series shot on film, which *revolutionized* the medium. It took him just a little time to forget the cameras and talk directly to me, the interviewer. He forgot about the bright lights and the microphone we had pinned to his lapel. He related wonderful stories of his early days in the new medium. And how he helped to shape the face of TV as we know it today. Goldenson appreciated the training. He thanked me, but riding in the limousine back to ABC, he told me that he still felt broadcast executives belonged behind the camera, not in front of it. *It doesn't mix well*, he said. I considered disagreeing, but decided pioneers deserved the last word. A few weeks later I moved over to NBC to join another pioneer, Fred Silverman. I didn't see Leonard again. But I heard he was a big hit on public television.

3

A Wind-Tossed Dollar Is Harbinger Of Millions

There have been a plethora of books lately that try to put a high-minded spin on public relations. A new book, *The Public Relations Handbook,* edited by Robert L. Dilenschneider, the former president of Burson-Marsteller, offers this highfalutin surrogate: *the art of influence.* But who's influencing whom? Sometimes we publicists are the ones being influenced. Or even duped. Recently we had our wrists slapped by *The Wall Street Journal* for distributing material that a client had provided us, which turned out to be false and misleading. When the *Journal* called the company on it, the client said they never authorized us to release such material. It was a clear case of shifting the blame onto the messenger. Because it manufactures a lock for firearms, we call this erstwhile client *the little company that couldn't shoot straight.* Today we require clients to accept full responsibility for the accuracy of material they want us to distribute. We also have them sign an agreement holding us harmless if it's not. And everything we send out must have their approval in writing. Another time the art of influence backfired, wounding me and a few of my closest friends.

I was promoting one of the ventures of that entrepreneurial genius, Rocky Aoki. When Rocky first stepped foot onto U.S. soil from his native Japan, a dollar bill blew across the tarmac right up to his pants leg. He scooped it up and put into his pocket. *My parents always told me America's streets were paved with gold, but they never said anything about hard currency,* Rocky would quip later after his entrepreneurial spirit took flight and his fortunes soared in this new country. That wind-tossed dollar was a harbinger of millions that would fly into his pockets after he created a new restaurant featuring samurai jugglers who diced, sliced and flipped your bean sprouts before your amazed eyes. Rocky created the brilliantly entertaining *Benihana.* His picture was on the cover of *TIME.* He spoke at the Harvard Business School. So who wouldn't be excited if Rocky let you in on one of his deals? I know I was.

And I told my friends Larry, Bill and Glenn who also invested in *Rocky Aoki's Japan Plan.* It was a collection of diet products, including diuretic herbal teas from the Pacific Rim, that would make you thin as a sushi chef. Rocky would wax entrepreneurial at nighttime meetings at his uptown Manhattan eatery off Avenue of the Americas, telling us how he planned to package it in a Pagoda Box and market it multi-level like Mary Kayota. *Have you ever seen a fat Japanese?* he'd ask rhetorically. Come to think of it, none of us ever had. So we invested in the private placement and were issued stock certificates by a blithesome character from Massapequa named Don Kessler, a crony of Rocky's, and columnist Dan Dorfman. Don said he could get Dorfman to do a favorable story on Rocky's newest venture. I was going to help publicize the new diet. And my friends were going to be grateful to me forever for making their bodies thin and their wallets fat. But it didn't quite turn out that way.

Kessler did nothing but sell shares of stock. We never saw our first Pagoda Box. Rocky and Kessler had a penchant for gambling with other people's money and they both had terminal attention deficit disorder when it came to staying focused. When I confronted Rocky and asked who was setting up the manufacturing and distribution network for the Japan Plan, he held up a circular mirror about a foot in diameter. I wondered if this was the mother of all smoke and mirror tricks.

"I want to put at intersections across country, like in Japan," he said. "When you drive up to street corner, mirror lets you see cars coming on cross street. You slow down. Work very good. Stop accidents. You want to help promote?"

"No thanks," I said. "What about the Japan Plan?"

"I don't know. Talk to Kessler. He's handling."

And that's the art of the deal sometimes. It goes back and forth, then south! Meanwhile, Larry, Bill, Glenn and myself still have in our portfolios shares of a once-promising company that I was going to promote called *Japan Plan, Inc*. I don't think you'll see it on the cover of *TIME*. And I never saw any mirrors on street corners either, until I moved to Palm Beach. There's a couple off A1A. And you know, they're not a bad idea.

A few years later, the Securities and Exchange Commission launched an investigation into allegations that a certain blithe spirit from Massapequa had sold access to Dorfman to company representatives. Dan said it wasn't true, but he lost his job at *Money Magazine* anyway.

4

Charging Like A Scimitar-Wielding Cossack

I f they're not calling public relations *the art of something,* they're putting such a redeeming *spin* on what we do for clients, it sounds as if we're working more for the public good than our clients' financial welfare. Then let this book be a sobering departure from such pompous patting ourselves on our back. And let's get realistic. We're here to make money for our clients. Period. End of News Release.

The corporate client today is focused on increasing profits quarter after quarter, not on doing good deeds. The refined public television program brought to you by the magnanimousness of Mobil Oil Corporation is giving way to Chain Saw Al Dunlap charging into a crowd of Scott Paper employees like a scimitar-wielding Cossack, cutting them down like so much tissue clogging up the flow of dividends to shareholders. If they do anything in the public interest, today's corporations want a pound of exposure for their ounce of giving. Even philanthropist David Rockefeller acknowledges that a company's first obligation is to be lean and mean before it can be kind. Before you give oxygen to a child when the pressure drops at 30,000 feet, you strap yours on first. And that, my friends, is telling it honestly, in terms that are practical, not cynical. I've been in enough board rooms to know what I'm talking about. Lest we become effete and irrelevant to what business and industry is all about, public relations needs to help companies move products and grow their businesses, or else we become a superfluous messenger. And the chain-saw cometh for us too.

Maybe this won't please the *Public Relations Society of America*, of which I'm an accredited member, but today's realities require a more sharply-focused definition of public relations. It's *the business of crafting communications to promote business.* Is there something wrong with disseminating self-serving messages? In business, it's the thing to do, unless you're suicidal.

Communications also can be measured on a color scale from the fiery red of propaganda to the snow white of *pure speak,* then off the charts to the transparency of *technitalk,* intended to be ultra clear and bias-free. But without tint, communications are dull and won't do the job of promoting business. Dab them with color and they become alive and effective. If there's any art to it at all, it's *the art of the tale.* But don't call it *PR.* My colleagues consider it a pejorative term. ie., *Does he mean it or is it just a lot of PR?* (Translation: Is it true or just bullshit?) As for myself, I kind of like the term.

Does coloring mean lying? I never condone lying to the press. Not only is it wrong, it's dangerous. Yet should we tell the whole truth? Often that's neither wise nor kind. Like telling your poor old aunt: *My what a big ugly wart you have on your chin!* What you do tell should be the truth, however. You might creatively stretch it, but I wouldn't call that lying. But telling the whole truth about our clients? No sirree! That could be costly to your career. And you cub reporters, listen up. Before we come to you, we've had plenty of sessions trying to decide which of our client's feet to put forward first. And which are best left in the closet. If you ferret them out, that's fine. Maybe you'll win your Pulitzer. More likely, you'll just dig up some smelly feet.

Larry Linderman, a longtime friend who wrote opera singer Beverly Sills' best-selling biography and more Q&A interviews for *Playboy Magazine* than any other writer, says I should tell you here how I got into public relations. But before I do, you should know a little more about me.

5

**I always had a great sense of timing, Henry...
when to give, when to take.**
—Oliver Stone's **NIXON**

I grew up in Atlantic City not far from the blue properties, Boardwalk and Park Place. This was prior to it becoming the gambling mecca it is today. Dean and Jerry were appearing at the 500 Club and stately old hotels like the Traymore still graced the Boardwalk, where my dad was musical director for 30 years. Nothing yet had been dynamited into a pile of rubble or replaced by light bulbs, shiny metal foil and neon. In those days, we didn't have a little red hotel on our property, just a row house on Bellfield Avenue between Kentucky and New York. But it was comfortable and a lot quieter than when we lived over Brooks & Idler Printing. And there was room for an office for my parents' business, The Convention Entertainment Bureau. Coming home from Catholic school with battle scars on my hands where the nuns had stung me with rubber bands in their never-ending war against my disruptive nature, I'd open our front door and enter paradise. It was a paradise populated by the leggiest, most magnificently endowed angels I'd ever seen. They waited to be interviewed to model or demonstrate or hand out complimentary cigarettes at Convention Hall with Dennis James and the tap-dancing packs of *Old Gold Cigarettes*. Atlantic City was the perfect place for a spin man to grow up. I learned the first step in any communications program—attracting people's attention. I saw visitors flock to see the diving horse at Steel Pier; gawk at Ed McMahon hawking steak knives from a kiosk on the Boardwalk; giggle at the Shriners in their fezzes riding miniature fire trucks; go for hair-raising rides on Captain Starn's speedboat; and partake of such cultural experiences as touring the insides of a wooden elephant. In its heyday, Atlantic City was a real *Spin City* that lived up to its slogan. It was *The World's Playground.*

My mom was a saver. Somehow she managed to squirrel away enough money from my dad's *entertainment allowance* so we could afford to move down to Ventnor into a duplex near Marvin Gardens. We lived upstairs and rented downstairs. Dad moved in the opposite direction, however, into an apartment in the Inlet, after my mother caught him two-timing her in Woolworth's with another woman. And he was giving this woman more than violin lessons at night. My mom cried herself to sleep, especially when dad had the nerve to take his floozy to the Hollywood Movie Theater where my mom cashiered, trying to save enough to send me to college. As sore as I was at my dapper dad for fiddlefaddling with other women, I missed watching his nightly ritual of getting ready to lead his salon orchestra at the Traymore Hotel. He'd pencil in his moustache, massage in green globs of *Dr. Elis' Wave Lotion* that made his black hair shiny and wavy stiff, dude up his shirt front, tie his bow tie, then slip into his regal tuxedo. Then everything changed. As a violinist he could tell that tremor years before any doctor could detect it. For *Bela* Madden, the "Irish gypsy violinist," the favorite and official gypsy violinist of King Carol of Romania, who had heard him play at Ciro's in Mexico City; the former first violinist of the Cleveland Symphony; the virtuoso who had mastered the intricate Paganini Concerto; the *bon vivant* of Galveston and Atlantic City; the dashing orchestra conductor and prestidigitator—my dad—had contracted Parkinson's disease. His belladonna medication made him mopey and clumsy. He put his violin back into its case for the last time, checked himself into a reclining chair, and watched TV until his heart gave out. Meanwhile, my mom took him back. It was heartbreaking to watch. I was in the first of my two-year run as a high school senior when my buddy Glenn and I decided to cheer ourselves up and catch some serious sun rays. So we played felony-level hooky and hitched a ride south with my Uncle Tony, who said he could get us jobs as pari-mutuel ticket sellers at Gulfstream Park. It turns out I landed in Florida with a much higher rank. I became a general . . . General d'Beauregard. Somehow I auditioned and won the part in George Bernard Shaw's *St. Joan* at the *Coconut Grove Playhouse*. I was young, saucy, semi-convincing. And I was ecstatic. The director said I had a remarkable sense of timing, a critique I would hear over and over again after college from acting teachers at the Herbert Berghof Studio in Greenwich Village. After seeing me play the *Boor* in Checkoff's one act play, Bill Hickey encouraged me to keep at it. Besides me, Hickey's students included Steve McQueen, George Segal, Sandy Dennis and Barbra Streisand. Years later Bill won an Academy Award nomination for his portrayal of the old Mafia Don in *Pritzi's Honor*.

Mr. Corleone Would Appreciate Your Space

Now please close the door. I wish to digress. We'll return to Florida in a minute. Come closer. The world doesn't need to know the family's business. After seeing *The Godfather* so many times, the idea of representing such a character has always intrigued me. Come closer. It's hard to talk with this cotton in my mouth. As I was telling Barzini only yesterday, can't you just see a PR guy handing a news release to a reporter. The spin man tells the reporter:

> "Mr. Corleone would appreciate your running this in your paper."

> "No, don't give me any stories. Who do you dago wops think you are? You can't push the press around."

> "Very well. If you refuse, I need to inform Mr. Corleone. For he is a man who insists on hearing bad news immediately. And excuse me for asking, but by any chance are you fond of horses?"

No, I've never represented any Goodfellows. And one of my clients, *The National Italian American Foundation*, despises *The Godfather* for feeding the stereotype that all Italians are gangsters. They'd like to get their hands on Coppola's master print. And stab it with an ice pick. Just joking NIAF.

But I did come close to the real thing once. And I ain't talking about no Coca-Cola. I will tell you about it. Come closer. One day I received a call from a man who said he represented someone looking for a PR guy. He couldn't give me the prospect's name, but he gave me a street address in an exclusive neighborhood in Queens. I recognized the neighborhood.

New York City's disgraced comptroller had just stabbed himself fatally with a kitchen knife in his home there. Now before we go any further, you must realize that it's not uncommon for prospects to want to conceal their identify while they're shopping for PR help. Often companies wish to remain anonymous so not to tip off anyone that there's going to be an acquisition or some other development that's going to generate publicity. People who are in trouble also hire PR firms as trouble and crisis often breed legitimate work for PR professionals like myself. So the caller gives me a time when this cloaked party would like to see me. My wife thought it sounded ominous and I shouldn't go. But I just wanted to find out who it was, I told her. And the next night I drove out to Queens.

The address I had been given was a large corner home. When I rang the front door bell, a stocky, round-faced man wearing a dark blue sport shirt opened the door a quarter of the way. When I gave my name, he opened it the rest of the way and motioned for me to come inside. I entered a vestibule, where he told me to wait. He returned with two other men wearing sport jackets. *You the PR guy?* one of them asked. *Yeah,* I answered. Normally I'd say *Yes I'm Tom Madden, how do you do?* But *yeah* seemed to fit the situation better.

Then they said to follow them and I was led into a living room where an older gentlemen was sitting on a sofa. He invited me to sit down and watch a videotape. One of the men who had escorted me into the room, inserted a tape into the machine and hit the play button. When it started to play, I saw TV news clips of John Gotti, the Teflon Don himself, climbing the stairs of the courthouse. For years Gotti had cut a lively figure as a chic mob godfather, dashing around town in limousines from trendy restaurants to night clubs, to racetracks, to walk-and-talk meetings in Little Italy. Then the news coverage switched to scenes of a City Council meeting. Now the reporter was talking about a contract the city had with a plumbing firm that employed Gotti.

When the tape ended, the old gentlemen erupted into a tirade. *That's the bullshit I want stopped. They're killin' my business. John and I grew up together. So I gave my boyhood friend a job. So what? What's so wrong with that? Now the city won't do no more business with me. It's costing me millions of dollars in work. I need PR. I don't* care what it costs. You name a figure.

Few times in my life I've been speechless. This was one of them. So I retreated behind a question to gain time to recover my wits. *What does Mr. Gotti do for you? He's in sales. And he's damn good.* That I could believe. He was probably the kind of salesman you just couldn't refuse. I tried to think of a PR strategy, but all that would come up was his disassociating immediately from the celebrated don. But I could just hear my wife. *Oh that was nice. You recommended firing the Godfather!* I told the older gentleman that I wanted to think about it. Could I get back to him tomorrow? He said okay. And I got out of there fast as I could.

Next day, I phoned him and said I didn't feel I was the right PR person for him as I specialized in a different area of public relations. Whatever that meant. He said okay, and thank God, I never heard back. Since then, his boyhood friend went from the *Teflon Don* to the *Velcro Don.* The Federal charges all finally stuck. The Feds put Gotti away for life. For a while he continued to reign over the Gambino crime family from his tiny cell in a maximum security prison in Illinois.

But even that faded as leaders of the New York region's four other powerful Mafia families told the acting head of the Gambino family to replace Gotti. Since he was allowed out of his cell only an hour a day, he was finding it difficult to transmit orders. Needless to say, Gotti's plumbing sales had plummeted.

• • •

Playing a general at The *Coconut Grove Playhouse,* only 1,600 miles off Broadway, wasn't too shabby for a 17-year-old kid. Much later, after Glenn and I graduated from Temple University I would play another Shavian general—General Burgoyne in *The Devil's Disciple.* Off Broadway! At the rank I was going, I could have been the founder of the Epaulette School of Acting in New York, but my young Italian bride, Angela, wasn't very encouraging. She and my brother-in-law Nicky, a carpenter from Brooklyn, sat in the first row opening night, measuring my performance. Later that night she gave me my first taste of her unassailable Italian logic. *You keep this up and we're going to starve.*

Back in my thespian days in New York, I would've given anything to meet a Mark Schwartz.

6

Fools Rush In Where Wise Men Fear To Tread...

Nothing spins as sexy as a Broadway Show. No matter how promising the playbill, it's no investment for the faint of heart, however. But sit back and let me raise the curtain on *SCHMUCK*, a musical comedy based on a PR guy who trades a year's worth of his services for one percent of a new Broadway musical. The musical is *Dream*, based on tunes by lyricist Johnny Mercer, such as *Fools Rush In*. If I had to pay cash for that point, like other investors, it would have cost $70,000. Tryouts in Nashville and Boston so far have been a smash. *Dream* is scheduled to open on Broadway in April 1997. And if it runs as long as producers say it will, the returns are going to be incredibly *Goody, Goody*. And I'm excited, excited.

The scene opens in the luxurious waterfront home of Victoria Williamson. Assembled are Jean Van Waveren, a Palm Beacher who already has a stake in the musical; Victoria, her entourage and two servants who continually light her cigarettes and keep vigil over her bottomless champagne glass. Wherever she goes, they're the chorus line and she's the star of the revue. Pacing the perimeter of the living room containing a motley, hastily-gathered group of prospective investors and looking anxiously at his wristwatch is a man in about his mid forties. Lean and intense. Hair swept back into a pony tail. A short-cropped beard gives him a theatrical air. Right you are. He's the producer, Mark Schwartz. Winner of Tony Awards for *Nine, My One and Only* with Tommy Tune and Twiggy and *La Cage Aux Folles*. And now co-producing *Dream* with Louise Westergaard, a Tony winner for *Sophisticated Ladies*. At this moment, however, Mark's upset.

We're at a private, ultra exclusive *backer's audition,* sometimes called an *Angel's Party*, but people are drinking too much and it's taking too long for them to take their seats in the impromptu rows of chairs facing the piano. They're about to enjoy something very special and privileged. The cast, headed by the legendary songstress Margaret Whiting, has come all the way from New York to perform in this intimate setting. It's like a *road show* at which CEOs try to get money managers to invest, only with music.

Dream is a musical in five scenes which portrays Mercer's romantic and innocent America from the 1920s through the 1960s. Mercer won four Academy Awards for songs like *Moon River* and *Days of Wine and Roses* and was nominated 17 times. *Dream* combines the lyrics of the legendary lyricist and composer, with music by the greatest writers of those decades—Jerome Kern, Hoagy Carmichael, Duke Ellington, Henry Mancini and others. The sets and costumes are based on creations by art deco artist Erte. Thirteen characters reappear in decade after decade, each playing their prototypical roles of ingenue, vamp, leading man, etc. as shaped by the changing circumstances of each era. The overall effect is a dream-like collection of memories. But for Mark this backer's audition for *Dream* would be more like a nightmare.

Finally everyone staggers to their seats. The overture begins. And the audience is transported by an imaginary train to Savannah, Mercer's boyhood home as the cast sings *Goody, Goody*. Whiting and the others start taking turns singing such Mercer hits as *Come Rain or Come Shine, Blues in the Night* and *Fools Rush In*. But what's going on with this audience? Mark's getting livid. These rubes are getting up from their chairs and walking right in front of the piano—while the cast is singing their hearts out—and going to the bar for refills. And talking loutishly among themselves. Valiantly the performers ignore this disintegration of all decorum that's going on just a few feet in front of them. Somehow they keep the show on track and mercifully for them and Mark, they reach the finale . . . *Dream when you're feelin' blue, that's the thing to do* . . . it's Mark's cue to get ready to make the all-important pitch for the audience to put money into the show . . . *if you just Dream.* Applause. Mark's face is red and it's not from sunburn. But before he can reach the piano, Victoria rises unsteadily. She thanks the cast and her guests for coming and invites everyone to her new restaurant. Mrs. Van Waveren tells her to sit down and shut up. Victoria tells Mrs. Van Waveren: *It's my home. I'll do as I please.* Intoxicated angels start milling towards the bar. Margaret Whiting and the cast are outraged. Louise is furious. Mark's having palpitations. It was the worst possible ending of a backer's audition. Of course, no one invested. And to this day, Mark believes most of the people in Victoria's living room that night hadn't a clue what they were doing there, or what it was all about.

The one possible positive outcome was that my wife and I got to be friends with Mark. And we made this deal with him. Since he had moved to Palm Beach, we would generate publicity about him and his new musical throughout the region. The spin would be that Palm Beachers were backing Mark's new musical bound for Broadway, so there was a local rooting interest in its success. Mark signed a contract with us which provided that in return for our services, we would receive a one percent interest in the show, plus a finder's fee if we could drum up some investors. This wasn't *The Producers* with Zero Mostel. This was legit. So we got Mark some terrific stories in the local press. We booked him on local TV and got him invited to shindigs where he could meet the right people. Then one day, he phones us from New York. He says there are still a few units left to sell and could we get anyone to a backer's audition in Louise's apartment? I told him we'd scout around.

Then I heard that Bob Cuello was in Manhattan. He owns a bunch of car dealerships and loves the limelight. He'd be perfect to invite. So we called someone who knew him pretty well. We told her if she could get him to the backer's audition, we'd split our finder's fee with her. She agrees and calls Bob to give him the address and time. But knowing his phobia about everyone chasing him for money, she doesn't tell him it's a backer's audition. She says it's a party where he'll meet a lot of showbiz people. So Bob shows up. He's surprised at what he walks into, but falls in love with the show. And eventually he buys enough units to become its Associated Producer.

A month goes by. Two! Our friend inquires about her half of the finder's fee. So I call Mark. And I can't believe what he tells me. He says he's *troubled* over the finder's fee. He says Bob made him pledge that no one's receiving a commission on his investment. I remind Mark our deal is with him, not with Bob. Mark tells me it wasn't right to trick Bob into coming. He's *uncomfortable* we got Bob to the backer's audition under false pretenses. *It wasn't fair.* I remind this moralist that if Bob knew what he was going to, he would never have gone. And it wasn't me who deceived him. But what's the difference? We got him there. He invested. It wasn't *Bullets Over Broadway. No one put a gun to anyone's head. And you weren't forced to take his money. So when do we get the finder's fee?* In a couple of months, he says, and hangs up. So I've been waiting. It's been six months already. And frankly I'm starting to get the *Jeeper's Creepers.*

• • •

A couple years ago one of my idols, Jose Ferrer, became creative director of *The Coconut Grove Theater* shortly before his final exit. On behalf of The Fort Lauderdale Film Festival, I invited him to receive a lifetime achievement award. He was too busy to accept, so we gave it to Van Johnson instead. But who'll ever forget Jose as Cyrano de Begerac? I've always felt Cyrano is what South Florida needs, not Dr. Kevorkian . . . a Cyrano who can point his foil at all the retirees who've warehoused themselves in condos, waiting for death. Only Cyrano could tell them with such eloquence: *You shall die exquisitely.*

At night as a youngster playing General d'Beauregard I commanded the stage at *The Coconut Grove Theater.* During the day, I was in charge of a cabana at a Miami Beach hotel, where elderly men kept telling me my flies were open. They were wrong. They only seemed that way because the material in my groin area was always stretched in those days, which exposed the closed zipper. Even so, it was enough to draw derisive comments like "Whatta ya advertising?"

I realize now what I must have looked like to those testosterone-starved bulls out to pasture. Little did I know then that I'd one day be promoting experts in hormone replacement therapy. Are you satisfied, Harold? To this day I can't enter a room without checking my zipper.

7

Dance like a butterfly. Sting like a bee.
—Muhammad Ali

My background in media has definitely given me an edge in PR. I was the son of a gypsy violinist who didn't cotton much to music like his Irish dad dreamed, but rose instead to be vice president of a television network. My mother always prayed to St. Jude that I'd get a break. And I did. When I was 21, I broke my neck when I dove off a boat onto a sandbar. Friends would visit me in the hospital where I was hung for eight weeks suspended from hooks screwed into my head. And they'd tell me how lucky I was. For a couple of years after that I drifted aimlessly as mother made novena after novena and handed out her St. Jude prayer cards. St. Jude is the patron saint of lost causes. And for me, he was appropriate. Trying to find myself, I had gotten lost.

It would be years before I would be written up in *FORBES* and *TIME* . . . make WHO'S NEWS in *The Wall Street Journal* . . . become a biography in *WHO'S WHO IN THE EAST* . . . and a newspaper reporter and an interviewer of legends like Muhammad Ali. My career finally started to rev up when I became a reporter for *The Philadelphia Inquirer*. One of my first assignments was to interview that lyrical soul and unconquerable clown, Ali, the consummate put-on artist of pugilism at the height of his powers. When I got to Ali's home in Cherry Hill, New Jersey, which was not too far from our first home, he made me take off my shoes before inviting me inside. And then he took me on a personal barefoot tour around his sprawling 12-room house. Groups of people were behind practically every door he opened, which he closed right away. This was some time after he had danced like a butterfly and stung George Fraser with a beehive of punches and had vanquished the fearsome George Foreman in Zaire, regaining the title he'd been stripped of for refusing military service in Vietnam.

And I interviewed the top of officialdom, too, like President Nixon before he stung us all. He had come by train to Philadelphia to attend a concert at the Academy of Music. When I asked him how he liked the train ride, he treated me to a loquacious reply as mine had been the only question not about the Vietnam War which we were losing.

Later at the Academy of Music, next to the hotel made famous by Legionnaire's Disease, where I had sat on a bed with Sammy Davis Jr. interviewing him in his room about his experiences with racists and where once my mom and dad and I lived while he played the violin at the Bellvue Stratford, I heard shots ring out.

They sounded like they had been fired from the stage. *Oh my God*, I thought. I started to run toward the box where the President was sitting . . . images flashing in my head of Booth, Lincoln, my City Editor, my seventh grade teacher telling me I was lazy and didn't try hard enough. Could this be my Delea Plaza? My book depository? The big one? And I'm the only reporter within miles of maybe a mortally-wounded President . . . whose bloodied head I might have to cradle in my arms . . .Who confesses his role in Watergate to me as he lay dying . . . but I feel pain flare up my arms. Suddenly I'm on the floor. Someone's on top of me. Holding me from the story of the century.

> "Let me go. I heard shots. I'm a reporter," I yelled at the wires in their ears.
> "It's the '1812 Overture,' you schmuck," said one of the secret service men. "Cannon fire, it's in the music."

Why did Tchaikovsky have to humiliate me with his melodramatic fusillade? I deserved 40 lashes with horsehair from my father's bow. He used to joke he made a living sliding it over catgut. He did it for 30 years in the Traymore Hotel dining room. And for a few of those years he tried hard not to look at his son balancing weighty trays with one hand that were stacked precariously with dirty dishes, sailing over the heads of his audience.

So careful he was about his hands, I don't remember my father ever beating me, though he flailed at me once when I dropped the five-pound bag of Epsom Salts on his foot and couldn't stop laughing. And when I shot out the streetlights in Brigantine with my BB gun outside the bungalow while he practiced his Mendelssohn. I spent a good part of adolescence tiptoeing around that damn Mendelssohn Violin Concerto and the 12 string symphonies Mendelssohn wrote as a teenager for concerts in the family salon. *Shhhhh. Your father's practicing*! Other kids' fathers played ball with them. Mine fiddled while I burned. That violin was my step father. The next most important thing in my father's life was his El Producto Cigars, then his magic tricks, like the *incredible multiplying rabbits*. So in descending order his priorities were: violin, cigars, multiplying rabbits and me!

8

A Cupful Of Initiative

What propelled me that night at the Academy of Music was an early sign of a trait that once in a while got me into trouble, but mostly has served me well in PR. Resourcefulness! And it bloomed in a field of competition. But so many media markets today are becoming less competitive. Too many cities now have only one newspaper and virtually identical, homogeneous Six O'Clock and Eleven O'Clock local news programs. *Resourcefulness* and its companion *initiative* are becoming endangered species. I developed mine as a journalist trying to beat other reporters to the story. To this day I can't see people going into PR who haven't worked for a newspaper. How could you work in Paris if you can't speak French?

In Philadelphia, the competition was *The Philadelphia Inquirer* vs. *The Philadelphia Evening Bulletin*. And it kept you on your toes. Today, like so many afternoon papers, *The Bulletin* is gone, but when I started as a reporter, I was always racing to beat it to the story, like the time I was sent to cover the first skyjacking at Philadelphia International Airport. When I arrived, a police line blocked reporters as FBI agents were interviewing the released hostages being held in quarantine at one of the gates.

I spotted a waiter carrying pots of coffee. I ran over to him and told him to go get some more right away and that I'd take these into the hostages. I ran into a bathroom and, like Clark Kent, took off my tie and jacket, tucked my steno pad into my pants, took a deep breath and headed toward the police line holding up the coffee so the cops could see I was a waiter like my grandfather.

Hot coffee for the passengers, I said to the cops who let me through. *Did you see the skyjacker? Were you close to him? What did he look like?* I asked as I refilled the passengers' coffee cups. They were still too shook up to wonder why a waiter was asking so many questions and recording their juicy eyewitness accounts in his steno pad. Early that morning I phoned in one of the best stories I ever dictated, including a vignette about a professional wrestler on the plane who had helped to subdue the skyjacker. When they saw my bylined story on our front page that morning, the editors at the *Bulletin* nearly all had heart attacks en masse. And the TV crews who had been held behind police lines all night must have wanted to commit sepuku with their microphones.

At the *Inquirer,* I rose to general assignment reporter and feature writer, promoted up the ranks from a rookie. Those days you only needed to touch type on an electric typewriter and have the nerve to ask families for a photo of a loved one killed in Vietnam, which most provided proudly. And it helped to be daring or foolish, like the time I followed the fresh bloody foot prints of the cop killer into a home where he had sought refuge in North Philadelphia after ambushing two patrolmen in their police car . . . the chutzpa to interview Dr. Jonas Salk while pissing in the urinal beside him. He suggested we shake hands later. The turbulent 70s. Those were exciting times to be a reporter in a big city. Covering fires in North Philadelphia, I had to wear a steel helmet because of the snipers. Seconds after walking away from two fireman at a blaze in Conshohocken, a fiery wall collapsed, killing them both instantly. Even cops were a menace. One day I got punched by police officers and dragged into their station house in broad daylight after I asked one for his reaction to my story on police corruption.

To get that story I sat all night in a parked car in a tough South Philadelphia neighborhood with a female reporter. We embraced like lovers whenever someone looked suspiciously at us. (Angela, I swear it was in the line of duty.) And we observed cops taking bribes at a bookie joint. Being a reporter makes you resourceful, which is why I'm impatient with publicists who leave messages and sit around waiting for callbacks. I admire people who hustle, who keep trying different avenues. I never waited. I'd call someone's parents, employer, priest, rabbi or mistress. Anyone I could find who knew where they were. Or I'd go out looking for them. And usually I'd come back with a story. And it was this conditioning that enabled me years later in public relations to come back with an entire audience.

9

See The USA In Your (Alamo-Rented) Chevrolet...

The California desert was still dry and hot. But it was approaching dusk. And we were speeding out from LA to some remote location in the mountains where James Edward Olmos was shooting a movie. Tomorrow was the big news conference our PR firm had been preparing for several months. And when we arrived in LA from Florida, we found a message at our hotel saying that he was sorry, but he couldn't make it. But this was the launch of *The Alamo Rent A Car Film Competition For Students*. Alamo was a major client. And the President of Alamo was flying out to introduce Olmos, who had agreed to be one of the contest's advisors. We were driving out to persuade Eddie to take a break from his movie. He didn't have to drive in from wherever—he could join the news conference by satellite. There was only one problem. We were lost. My wife Angela calls 911 on our portable phone and says to the dispatcher: *We're from Florida and we're lost.* She said it that way for dramatic effect. It was 1993. And German tourists were getting shot to death after they had gotten lost in Florida . . . in their Alamo rental cars.

The dispatcher must have thought we made one hellova wrong turn. Anyway, he guided us to the address where Eddie was staying. We went to his motel room to see him. He greeted us warmly. We took him out to dinner and had a wonderful time. And he agreed to join the news conference the next morning by satellite. Only the next morning Eddie, Alamo and our entire event was upstaged dramatically . . . Dinah Shore died.

You could forget about the press. Every reporter in Hollywood was working on a retrospective on the legendary singer. So I took a different tack and called *Bloomberg,* the business wire service. I put a business spin on the story saying it was Alamo's new marketing strategy to rent more cars to the film industry. Bloomberg decided to cover it. A half hour before the conference, only a handful of Alamo's guests had showed up. And none of the film industry officials we had invited. Now we needed bodies for those empty chairs! Only ten minutes to go. Still not enough people. Frantically, I went out into the lobby of the hotel and started going up to people and inviting them to the conference. No one was interested.

Then I remembered the danish and coffee we had ordered. I made an announcement in the lobby. *Complimentary breakfast now being served in Meeting Room A.* I went throughout the hotel and repeated the announcement. People started to filter into Meeting Room A. It was almost 10 AM. We were up on the bird. And the room was packed. People were noshing danish and gulping coffee. I asked everyone to take their seats. They brought their danish and coffee to their seats. The President of Alamo delivered the speech we had written. He introduced Eddie who appeared via satellite on the giant screen right on cue.

Eddie was eloquent. And generous. He thanked Alamo for what it was doing to encourage young film makers. During the Q&A, the Bloomberg reporter asked wonderful questions. Afterward people came up and thanked me for the danish and coffee. Some even said they enjoyed the news conference. I thanked them for coming. There's nothing worse than empty seats. And finally I flopped down in one myself. Exhausted!

· · ·

Two Cuddly Clients: Attila And Cruella

As a footnote on the event, I almost didn't go. Shortly before we were to leave for LA, in the middle of launching this major PR program, I had to tell our clients at Alamo, in so many words, to go screw themselves. Now that sounds unprofessional as hell, doesn't it? But listen to the facts and see what you would have done. First let me introduce the characters in this next scene. To protect their real identify, as they both may be humbler now and in need of employment, we'll call them *Attila* and *Cruella*. But when we worked for them, they were both riding high. Attila is what you might call a full-figured woman in her thirties, but her round cherubic face makes you wonder if she lost 30 pounds, she could be Attila the Honey instead of the Hun. Nervous Cruella would be just as stout if she didn't drink 15 cups of coffee a day. By now her kidneys must be the color of used coffee grounds, though she's only been Alamo's Sergeant Manager of Community Relations for a couple of years. And her disposition runs from forced perfunctory in the morning to downright nasty by three 3 *PMS* every afternoon. So I receive a call from Cruella. And it sounds serious. And I wonder what could have gone wrong. She asks me to come in the next morning to see her and her boss, Attila, Alamo's Czarina of Public Affairs. And to come alone.

Now let me explain how our business is set up. My wife and I are the owners. We employ a small staff and because we run a tight ship, we're quite profitable. We've learned over the years you don't have to be big to be effective in PR. In fact, our *boutique* agency can run circles around the larger shops. For the most part, I do the schmoozing with clients and deal with the media. Angela keeps the books, does the payroll and generally keeps the office humming. And that's the way we work . . . as a team. Once we considered taking our firm public, but an underwriter told us we sounded too much like *a mom & pop operation*. So what's wrong with that? This mom & pop are pulling in nearly a million bucks a year. We live pretty comfortably on the ocean. We do as we please. And we have the luxury of telling clients we don't like to take a hike. So we decide to stay private. And grow the old-fashioned way—through revenues from fees. We like who we are. And we like to work together. And travel together.

Now don't get the idea Angela's only an accountant. She's much better than I am at working a room. At introducing people and making contacts. She happens to be the best public relations person you'd ever want to have represent you. Bright. Quick. Experienced. And poised. If she has a flaw, it's that she's so personable, she sometimes upstages the dullards in this business who often are on the client side. These are PR people who fancy themselves as important executives. And they can have superior attitudes that are totally out of place in public relations. But Angela is comfortable rubbing shoulders with anyone, from the least among us to the mightiest. I used to marvel at the way she could chat with Fred and Kathy Silverman up in the RCA jet as we streaked across the country calling on NBC stations. Or with hundreds of buyers at a trade show where her vitality alone could light up any exhibit booth.

Sadly, I never got a chance to meet my wife's parents, who both died much too young. The main impression I have of them comes from yellowing photographs. One shows a dashing, mustachioed artillery officer in the Italian Army. His serious expression belies a reputation of being a jovial person and a kidder like his son, my brother-in-law Nicky. Michele LoBasso was a sculptor. He was a handsome, elegant man. And he and his lovely bride Santa were deeply in love with each other when the war tore them apart. Angela was just a child when her soldier father died at age 27 from pneumonia. At his burial with military honors during World War II, Santa tried to throw herself into his grave. Angela was a war casualty herself. Still melancholy over the death of her beloved husband, Santa got involved with an itinerant merchant, Giuseppe Milano. He was a smooth-talking traveling salesman who rode a bicycle from town to town in Southern Italy selling material from parachutes salvaged from assaults by U.S. Paratroopers near Naples. Santa was a strikingly beautiful, dark-haired seamstress, who used the silky white fabric to make wedding gowns. Her precocious five-year-old daughter, Angelina, helped her to sew Giuseppe's fabric, which was perfect material to making the light billowy gowns. Angela was five and a half when Santa married the parachute peddlar, only to find out too late that he was an alcoholic. It would be a tragic mistake.

Soon tension developed between Angela and her stepfather that would explode into abuse and misery, particularly when he came home drunk and mistreated her mother. And to this day it has left deep scars. So Santa, which means *saint*, brought her sensitive and unhappy daughter to the nuns to be raised with the other misfortunate children orphaned by the war. And Angela grew up in the convent in her hometown of Giovinazzo, a small fishing village on the Adriatic north of Bari. Her stepfather proceeded to give her mother a brood of kids and a hard life.

At age 11, Angela left the convent and once again tried to live with her mother and stepfather and her half brothers and sisters in a tiny mountain village to where they had moved in Southern Italy. But once again she had to be separated from her abusive stepfather.

Angela moved back to Giovinazzo to live with her grandmother, Savina, a sweet, hardy woman who worked long hours in the olive groves that thrived in the arid, reddish-clay-covered region known as Puglia. Savina had immigrated to the U.S. in 1919, which is the title of the poignant Claudio Villa song. But when the Great Depression began obliterating jobs for immigrants, Savina had returned to Italy with her daughter Santa. Santa was born in the U.S. Years passed. And in 1955, while I was still in high school in Atlantic City, far across the sea, Santa was realizing that time was running out for her daughter to keep her U.S. citizenship, which she herself had forfeited by voting for that traitor Mussolini. The rules required that a person born of a U.S. citizen in a foreign country must go to America before the age of 16 or lose their U.S. citizenship. Santa also wanted her bright, devoted daughter to have a better life in America. So she sent Angela off to America when she was 15 and a half by herself, just as she had sent her son, Angela's older brother, Nicky. I wish I could have greeted my future wife when she arrived the first time at the Port of New York wearing her red dress and faux white pearls and unable to speak a word of English. But it wasn't the time yet. Angela moved in with her grandmother who also had returned to America to be reunited with her long-lost husband. Savina had lost track of him for nearly 40 years and had presumed he was dead until a friend ran into him on a street in New York. Depressions, wars, transatlantic travel and poverty could do things like that to the families of immigrants.

At first, Angela tried hard to like America, but she couldn't help missing her native land, her mother and her kindly uncles and aunts in *Provincia di Bari*. But dutifully, she attended school in New York City and worked hard in a sewing factory up in the Bronx, where she rose to a managerial position. When she was 19, she decided to return to her native Italy and, with the money she had saved, find her mother a better apartment. Perhaps finally they could live together happily. Then a bureaucratic miracle occurred. A petition that she and her brother had filed to restore her mother's U.S. citizenship was granted. So immediately she stopped looking for an apartment and booked passage on a ship to America for her mother and her three half sisters and two half brothers. Thankfully her stepfather elected to remain in Italy. At first they all moved into Nicky's row house in Brooklyn, where the kids practically wrecked the place. When Nicky married, they moved to 119th Street in Manhattan, where Angela moved in with her grandmother and her mother and half brothers and sisters moved into another apartment on the same street. Then Santa's husband came from Italy and moved in with them and her mother's life became miserable again. The drinking and abuse resumed until one day it ended tragically. Santa hurled herself out of a window onto 119th Street.

· · ·

When I met Angela, she was 24 and about to put quarters in a juke box in a trendy uptown bar on Second Avenue. She was beautiful standing there with her long dark hair and her high cheek bones catching the light off the flashing machine. And when I heard her Italian accent, I was a goner.

"What would you like to hear?" I asked her as I put a bunch of quarters in.

"Are there any Italian songs?"

"Why? Are you from Italy?"

"Yes."

"So am I. Born in Italy. Absolutely. SÌ."

"You're kidding, you weren't born in Italy."

"Oh no?" (I recite a poem I had learned in college.) "Tanto
    gentile and tant'oneste pare la donna mia."

"That's beautiful. What is it?"

"It's a poem by Dante."

"You speak Italian well."

Even without having located Dean Martin's *Volare*, my heart was
soaring to the clouds. I couldn't take my eyes off Angela. And she was
looking into mine and smiling. She told me afterward that it was my
hazel eyes that attracted her. Hers were like shiny black olives. And I
could feel them in the pit of my stomach. Then her blonde girlfriend
Blanche comes over and nudges her.

"Let's go."

"No, you go ahead. He's taking me home."

I nearly look around to see who *he* was. But she's pointing at ME! And
she's beaming like I never saw a woman beam before. It was incredible. I tell Barry and Bill I'll see them later. And we rush out the door
into the chilly night and jump into a warm cab. She tells the driver to
take us to 119th Street and First Avenue. That's Spanish Harlem! But
sitting with this Italian beauty in the back seat, I didn't care if it was
East Berlin, the South Bronx or the Bolivian jungle. She told me she
was the manager of a sewing factory in the Bronx. She lives with her
grandmother. And when she came to America. And how her father
died. And she was raised in a convent because she couldn't get along
with her step father. She talked the entire way. And enchanted, I listened to every divinely accented word. And then the taxi arrived on the
street where she lives and where few guys of my color seldom walk at
night. And wonder of wonders in the 60s, she pays the driver.

We walk into her seven-story walk-up apartment building where she
lives on the fifth floor. On one of the flights up, we step over a drunk
asleep on a landing. Many of the green apartment doors have either

crucifixes or pictures of the Blessed Virgin on them. And signs in Spanish I can't understand. She keeps smiling at me. Holding my hand. Leading me up. When we reach her floor, she throws her arms around me and kisses me hard and passionately. I feel her body press against me, pushing me into the railing. It was wonderful. Breathtaking. Madonna, did I hit numbers! I was just starting to get into it when suddenly she pulls away. *Chiama me, tesora,* she says and disappears inside her apartment.

We went out the next night. And the next. And the next. During the week, she'd skip work and come to my bachelor pad in Brooklyn near Prospect Park. She'd bring me these incredible Italian sandwiches. But first we made love. And then we ate. And then we made love again. And ate again. I was studying acting. And this was like being in an Italian film. But I wasn't sure if acting was what I wanted to do. But Angela knew what she wanted.

She was focused and direct about it. Next to her, I was aimless. She seemed two or three centuries more mature and wiser than me. And she was so womanly. And motherly. *I want to be like a little mother to you,* she would tell me. And I kept thinking *Hey, hold on there, honey. I'm from New Jersey. Girls didn't talk that way in New Jersey. Or kiss like that.* But she knew what she wanted. Me! *Aimless!* So what happens when *aimless* meets *focused?* You know what happens. The human race happens. And four months later, a judge married us in Manhattan. And armed with a mop, soap, a bucket, sponges and an ironing board, Angela moves into my one-room apartment. And soon it's sparkling clean. And brighter than I ever imagined it could be.

Three months later on a freezing cold night on December 10, 1964, we were married again at Holy Rosary Church on 119th Street, across the street from where she had lived with Savina Lasorsa. At the climactic moment at the altar, I dropped the engagement ring and it rolled down past the coffin in the center aisle awaiting the next morning's funeral Mass. My parents, her brother Nicky and the small group of Angela's relatives and friends watched in horror as I chased the ring down the nave to the rear of the church. Thirty-two years later I gave my betrothed a five-carat, pear-shaped diamond that dwarfed the diamond she wore all those years. So my advice to young couples contemplating marriage is this: If the ring rolls past the casket, it's good luck.

So I go to see Atilla and Cruella, who in my opinion are snobs who couldn't hold a candle to my Angela when it comes to PR. Instead of winning people over like Angela could, they'd turn them off with their busy officiousness and superior attitude. And soon as I sit down in Attila's office, Cruella hits me with it:

> "We don't want Angela working on this news confer-
> ence. She's welcome to come as your wife to any of
> the social events, but we don't want her working at the
> table for us."
>
> "Why not?"
>
> "She's not Alamoized."
>
> "She's not what?"
>
> "Alamoized. You know, our particular way of doing things
> here at Alamo. Angela hasn't been involved with us as
> much as you have. She doesn't know Alamo's style. And
> our management frowns on husbands and wives working
> together." Translation: Angela's not white bread like us.

And Attila and Cruella had no concept of what it was like for a husband and wife to work together. Attila's husband was a pest control man. Cruella's sold boats. And if Alamo's corporate culture disapproved of husbands and wives working together, maybe that's why the company was losing millions of dollars. They didn't know how to be a family. And Angela was outgoing. Personable. She'd take press people by the arm over to meet our clients. That was too forward for Attila and Cruella. They had a more somber, funereal view of their role in the corporation. They thought being professional meant being reserved, businesslike and smug. And that they should keep a proper distance from press. Or, for that matter, from anyone not *Alamoized.*

These were hard-driving executive women striving to carve a niche for themselves, trying to get ahead in a male-dominated company. But in trying so hard to please robotic men, they had become robotic women. They thought they should be self controlled and super serious. Keep a dignified low profile. And this view clashed with Angela's vivaciousness, attractiveness and good nature. Angela didn't fit their image. She was warm. Friendly. They were cool. Calculating.

They were a pair of insecure, perennially-dieting, thoroughly *Alamoized* caffeine addicts. And they were in charge of the most human area of any business—public relations. And their worst fears were justified. Angela could run PR rings around them.

> "But Angela is involved in everything our firm's involved in. She is an owner. My partner."
>
> "Look, we're the client. Any agency would switch personnel around if a client had a problem with someone. All we're asking is that you respect the wishes of your client."
>
> "Yes, but we're not just any agency. And Angela isn't just any employee."
>
> "Well, that's the way we feel."
>
> "Then I quit. You can handle the news conference yourselves. If Angela doesn't go, I don't go."
>
> "You're giving us an ultimatum?"
>
> "I'm telling you that if Angela doesn't go, count me out."

The next day the two PR executives backed down. Angela said that after this news conference she wanted to resign the account. And much to Attila and Cruella's surprise, we did just that immediately upon our return from LA. About a year later, Attila and Cruella were no longer with Alamo. And a year later the company was sold to a mom and pop. Marti and Wayne Huizenga.

10

Punched Into Another Line Of Work

Ithought only boxers got punched into another line of work. But it happened to me at a rally of black militants in West Philadelphia. It wasn't too long ago that Malcolm X had said *I charge the white man as the greatest murderer on earth.* And that seemed to be the general feeling as I was the only white reporter covering a meeting where this demagogue was whipping up the crowd, blaming every problem in the black community on *whitey*. And as he harangued, a young black *actifist* came up and punched me in the mouth so forcefully it knocked me down. If you've never had the experience, let me tell you it's a spine-tingling, humbling, momentous event. And it can also be jarringly insightful. One minute you're standing there fully alert doing your thing and then *KABOOM*, you're sitting on the floor stunned, embarrassed and serenely bewildered. You feel a trickle of salty liquid running down your chin and suddenly deeply-concerned faces are hovering.

It shakes you into a new perspective on who you are, what you're doing and what in the hell happened! The next day I'm looking in the mirror at my broken front tooth and decide to try an easier line of work. I dug up the letter I had received from a journalism department chairman at Loyola University in New Orleans. He had read my Master's Thesis on *Editor Authoritarianism* published in *Journalism Quarterly*. In the study, I tested editors on an authoritarian scale and then had them rate hypothetical stories according to news value. The more authoritarian they were, the more likely they were to play up stories involving *non-conformists* or as we used to call them, *hippies*. Personally, the authoritarians were a mild mannered sort, but with pencil in hand they were Genghis Khan. The longer the hair, the scruffier the clothes and demeanor, the bigger was the headline. I interpret it as *We'll show those scurvy characters*. They had internalized media's role of upholding the status quo. And they were holding up *hippy* behavior for censure and ridicule.

So the department chairman invites me down, takes me on a tour of the campus and *French Quarter* and treats me to a lavish dinner at the St. Charles Hotel topped off by a slice of Mile High Ice Cream Pie. I was sold.

Teaching really wasn't that new to me. During the Watergate Hearings, I had students at Rutgers University write news stories based on each day's proceedings. And for scholarly credentials, I had a Master's Degree from The Annenberg School of Communications at University of Pennsylvania, a school endowed to redeem an Ambassador's dad's ex-con past. It was across from The Wharton School at America's oldest university founded by penny-wise Ben Franklin, whose solitary figure looms over Philadelphia. So I accepted the teaching position at Loyola. It was the 1970s and I was in my early thirties. We went to live lazily on the lakefront in the City That Care Forgot. In three years, my belly looked like a *Crescent*. I was an overweight Odysseus caught in *Cerci's enchantment*. Her red beans 'n rice. Her po'boys, crayfish and oysters. I rode my bike to campus. Students kept telling me how right I was, how clever I was. But career-wise, I was atrophying. Then one day the spell wore off. The Jesuits decided not to grant me tenure as an assistant professor of journalism. It was like a refreshing punch in the mouth.

As advisor to the campus newspaper, I had allowed students to publish an investigative report on alcohol consumption on campus. The series caused a furor among parents who were footing high tuition bills to shield their children from such devil's brew. But my students found the campus awash in booze and some students were on the path to early-stage alcoholism. It was too much truth for even Jesuits to bear. But it shook me out of my malaise. With three children and a job in jeopardy, I was forced to do what millions of workers do today—forget about job security, focus on what other skills I had to offer. And prepare to shove off.

You could say I'm a late, late, late, late, late, late, late, late, late, late, late, late BLOOMER! And crossroads can provoke insight! I saw that the single thread running through my life was communications. I had been an actor, a journalist and a teacher. How could I combine those skills in a good-paying job? Then it hit me. It was PR. So I looked up my future in the classified section of *The New York Times*. Through those columns, one of the country's largest public relations firms extended a hand to me. We sold our mortgage. Packed our belongings on the roof of our Fiat station wagon. And made the trek back to New York. And I was assigned to promote three wonderful clients: *Snap, Crackle* and *Pop*.

Back in those days, the government was trying to break them up, along with the entire cereal industry. The Justice Department charged it was a bloated oligopoly, stifling competition and ripping off consumers with artificially high prices. Thrust into the media glare, Kellogg's Company executives needed help in making their case to the national media. So I was dispatched out to Battle Creek, Michigan, to media train their top executives. And then one of those lucky breaks occurred. *The New York Times* decided to reprint a speech I had written for Kellogg's then- president Bill LaMothe. Nothing that significant had happened to a Battle Creeker in a long long time. He was so appreciative he flew to New York in his private jet to personally thank me. I was summoned to join him at the Plaza Hotel, where naturally we met over breakfast. After some friendly small talk over our cereal bowls, his conversation turned surprisingly solemn.

He declared it was the goal of his presidency to get more raisins into Kellogg's Raisin Bran. I searched his face for a sign of humor, but this

Battle Creeker wasn't kidding. This man was on a mission. You could say it was his *raisin d'etre*. Years later his determination paid off. He rose to Chairman. Much more importantly, he reached his summit: *Two scoopfuls in every box of Kellogg's Raisin Bran.*

The firm I had gone to work for was Dudley Anderson Yutzy Public Relations (pronounced *Youtzy*, not *Yutzy*). It was located on the corner of 57th & Avenue of the Americas, a few blocks north of ABC and NBC where my meteoric career would later take me. D-A-Y was an all-food agency. The place smelled of cooking. They had a large kitchen in the center of the agency staffed by nutritionists in lab coats. They were deadly serious as they experimented with recipes, which we had to taste test practically every day. D-A-Y's accounts were a Who's Who in the food industry: The Florida Citrus Commission, The Chocolate Manufacturers of America (we booked the "The Chocolate Lady" on talk shows), the Monosodium Glutamate Association (they gave us a headache), The Banana Growers Association and The Idaho Potato Commission. I took Idaho's governor Cecil Andres to dinner at a posh East Side restaurant where (oops) they served Long Island Potatoes.

A Royal Spin

Fir a brief time, I tried being a society publicist. I regard it as my unctuous period as I fancied myself a kind of courtier oozing with manners and charm that would endear me to wealthy women. I helped a princess add glamour and sizzle to her Rita Hayworth Gala at the Pierre Hotel in New York by recruiting Joanne Woodward as a co-honoree with actor Richard Kiley, who had starred in a TV movie in which Ms. Woodward portrayed a victim of disease. I also got FAO Schwartz to donate giant stuffed animals which turned lots of heads along Park Avenue sticking out of my convertible as I drove them up to the Pierre to be auctioned off. And it gave me two of my most embarrassing moments in PR.

One was when I was drafted to retrieve a fur coat. I had to go to Tammy Grimes' Manhattan apartment to fetch a luxurious Fendi fur she couldn't pay for. It was even more embarrassing for her. I was the undertaker coming to claim the furry body. She apologized profusely for being the high bidder at $32,000 the previous night as she handed it over. The Fendi sisters had donated the fur to be auctioned off to raise funds for Alzheimers. But Unsinkable Molly Brown sank the *live* auction when she confessed the next day that she could not afford the item and was just trying to run up the bidding to help Alzheimers. When I saw her heart was in the right place, I felt like a Catholic state trooper ticketing Mother Superior. The moral is if you drink, don't drive and for God's sake, don't bid at auctions.

Then one day I revealed my gaucheness. Like an idiot, I darted after a grape that had fallen from Princess Yasmin Aga Khan's plate during an afternoon tea party in her luxurious Central Park West apartment. The errant grape had dropped on the floor and rolled toward the door behind which Rita herself sat in eerie silence. When I returned it to her highness, she bade me put the grape down. She no longer wanted it. From this experience I learned a valuable lesson. Whenever a client drops food on the floor, just let it lay there.

11

I do not make extravagant claims for my medicine. If a person is already dead, for instance, there is only a slim chance that my medicine will do him any good.
—The Inspector General

Today our clients are a new breed. We've come a long way. From cream cheese schmears to skim milk'n organic honey. So you can see what I've gotten myself into, I'd like to introduce you to some current clients. I'll assemble them for you. Put them all together in a room, so to speak, so you can meet them. Let's say they all came in one day—as nightmarish a thought that is. They're waiting in the reception area. You be the judge. Tell me if I'm wrong to represent this motley group. To promote them and their panaceas. They constitute a whole new roster of clients we're promoting, and they rally around a banner called alternative medicine. Whatever you think of alternative medicine, it's a wellspring of remedies on which Americans spend more each year than on all the prescription drugs from all of the pharmaceutical companies in the country combined. And today I'm promoting them. And doing well promoting wellness. Yet who are these people? And are we right to publicize them and promote their products?

Reader, I want you to contain your skepticism for the next few pages. For what I'm about to describe to you, I didn't make up. I couldn't have. I'm not as imaginative as the clients of our Florida-based PR firm. Meet the pioneers we're promoting these days. The developers and marketers of the world's most popular products. Listen to their herbivorous hype, the phantasmagoria of their claims, pitches and beliefs. Catch the fervor of an evangelical movement; the zeal, maybe chicanery, of spiritual revivalists in a crusade against infidels snacking on potato chips and Reese's Peanut Butter Cups. I'm talking about alternative medicine, that emerging utopia that is part science, part circus, part marketplace and part Mecca. Here are actual testimonials in 1996 about the effects of a new wild yam cream excerpted from a nationwide teleconference call for independent distributors of this "incredible" new product:

> *My mother took 17 shots of estrogen so she wouldn't have a miscarriage with me in the 50s and now in the 70s I developed an estrogen toxicity. And one of the reasons women have problems is we have too much estrogen and not enough progesterone and, of course, I was born toxic with estrogen from those shots in utero, and so I had the worst menstrual cramps. My son called me the 'bitch from hell.' And nothing, no amount of narcotics, would work or take the pain away.*

> *When Mary approached me I too was skeptical because I had tried everything and nothing worked. And in the first cycle I could have PMS with no aspirin. I mean the first time in 44 years. So it was a miracle for me. So if it could work for me, the worst case, it would certainly work for everyone else. So I can't tell you how it has totally changed my life.*

Another *excited* user of wild yam cream had this to share:

> *I've always had really severe PMS since I was a teenager and I think one of the reasons it has been severe is because*

I'm hypothyroid; in other words I don't produce enough hormones. So I'm always sluggish, not much energy, prone to weight gain and irritability and such. So when I saw that this product could possibly help with that, I started using it. The very first hour, I called Beth, I'll never forget this, and I bet she doesn't either. "What in the world is in this stuff? This is incredible." I just had an enormous amount of energy. I mean I couldn't believe it. From a cream! And I felt so happy.

Not content with consuming a myriad of vitamins, minerals, herbs, ointments, tonics, homeopathic remedies and chiropractic cures, legions of Americans today are joining the swelling ranks of Amway-type multi-level marketers. They're marching bravely into the nutritional wasteland . . . holding high their banners of *Anti Aging*, *All Natural* and *Organic* . . . sharing their miraculous health experiences and related financial opportunities . . . converting flabby, fiber-deficient heathens and Big-Mac-pagans to their religion . . and reviving the rejects and human wreckage from corporate downsizings. If these poor souls have only a flicker of life left in them, their products will fan that flicker into a roaring fire of health and wealth.

12

Jewish Penicillin Makes Front Page

The first alternative medicine I ever promoted was chicken soup. Our 1986 campaign was such a hit with New York media that the *Public Relations Journal* gave it a rave revue. According to the esteemed trade journal of our profession, I had put together a public relations program that came off like a well-crafted three-act play. I had written the script, pulled together an incredible cast and taken my seat in the director's chair.

I have to hand it to my troupe. Everyone played their part superbly. Staging couldn't have been better. It blew the lid off the soup pot. It worked. And my script became known as the Great Chicken Soup War. The *Journal* called it *a farcical mini-epic that pitted a small delicatessen, 100 grandmothers and Henny Youngman against the makers of one of the country's best-selling cold remedies—Contact.*

The way the *Journal* depicted it, the play went something like this:

ACT 1—THE SET-UP
SCENE I

(AT RISE, The PR playwright himself is at home watching television. On the screen, a comedian named Steve Landesberg is comparing chicken soup to Contact cold capsules. Landesberg claims Contact is more effective than chicken soup for combating colds. Commercial ends.)
(Darkness.)

ACT I, SCENE II

(Ben's Best Kosher Deli on Queens Boulevard, in Queens, New York. Yours truly and the owner, Jay Parker, are sitting at a table, bowls of chicken soup in front of us.)

> **ME**: *Listen I've got a terrific idea. It won't cost much and you'll get a million dollars worth of publicity out of it.*

PARKER: (his feelings truly hurt): *They really said that? How could they say that? How can a simple pill compete against a good bowl of chicken soup?*
(Darkness.)

ACT I, SCENE III

(The set of *The Today Show* at NBC where I was once VP. Weatherman Willard Scott, a national spokesman for Contact, is battling the flu. As Scott sneezes and coughs—trying to report the weather while sick can be a difficult task—my wife Angela brings him a bowl of Ben's Best chicken soup. All over America, millions of TV viewers watch Scott—remember now, he is the national spokesman for Contact—gratefully sip from the bowl.)
(Darkness.)

ACT II—THE PROTEST
SCENE I

(Ben's Best Kosher Deli, February 18, 1986. Present are myself, Patricia Marcus, the account supervisor at our firm, TransMedia Public Relations [she used to do PR for Ringling Bros. Circus] and Parker. Also present—invited by us—are Congressman Gary Ackerman, comedian Henny Youngman, a number of local grandmothers carrying placards protesting Contact and a plethora of journalists.)

> **YOUNGMAN:** (holding bowl of soup): *Take my wife, please—but don't take this bowl of chicken soup! (Sips soup.) My mother used to put a secret ingredient in her soup. She used to say, 'If you eat my chicken soup for 100 years, you'll live to be a ripe old age.'*

(Journalists scribble notes frantically, flashbulbs pop.)

> **REP. ACKERMAN:** (reading from a proclamation): *Let it be known to all assembled that Ben's Best Kosher Deli . . . has courageously upheld the dignity, the honor, and the medicinal value of chicken soup, in the face of unwarranted and slanderous attacks from the slick, the cynical and the manipulators of Madison Avenue.*

(Journalists scribble notes frantically, flashbulbs pop.)

> **PARKER:** *Chicken soup is the drug of choice of all these grand-mothers . . . After all, there's no warning label, and we know what the side effects are over a 500-year period.*

(Journalists scribble notes frantically, flashbulbs pop.)
(Darkness.)

ACT III—THE RECONCILIATION
SCENE I

(Ben's Best Kosher Deli, February 24, 1986. Present are myself, Marcus, Parker, Congressman Ackerman, who knows a good thing when he sees one—an assortment of grandmothers, and the same plethora of journalists. Press coverage to date—an item on the front page of *The Wall Street Journal,* prominent coverage in *USA Today, The New York Daily News, Newsday* and other publications—adorn the walls of the delicatessen. Enter Willard Scott and representatives of SmithKline Beckman and BBD&O, the advertising firm that created the Landesberg commercial. Members of the delegation carry signs that read: 'Contact loves chicken soup!' and 'Contact and chicken soup are perfect together.' Willard Scott kisses each and every grandmother present, slurps soup.)

JEREMY HEYMSFELD, Contact spokesman: *We love chicken soup. But when we have a cold, we take Contact. And so do our grandmothers.*

(Journalists scribble notes frantically, flashbulbs pop.)
(Darkness.)

CURTAIN

EPILOGUE

ME: *We did this to show what can be done for a relatively small client—it benefitted Ben's Best and gave us a chance to show what we can do.*

PARKER: *We weren't unpopular or unknown before we did this, but there have definitely been pay-offs. For example, we've been approached about labeling our own chicken soup. Nothing's signed, sealed, and delivered, but the lawyers are talking, and we owe it all to TransMedia. What I want to know is, What are they going to do for me next week?*

13

Sweet Sundays At Gram's

Back in those carefree, Chock-Full-Of-Nuts days of the 70s and early 80s, organic food meant mottled produce, granola and maybe a bottle of carrot juice. Herbal tonics and alternative medicine were the stuff oddballs went in for. And I was no oddball. Order *organic fettucine Alfredo* in Little Italy and you might get a bullet in your throat like Stirling Hayden got in *The Godfather*. No, I was as mainstream as you could get in those days; I was in advertising promoting healthy name brands like *Kent Cigarettes with the Micronite Filter*. I had worked my way up from the mailroom at Lennen & Newell Advertising on Madison Avenue to *Creative Research*.

Little did I know I was persuading people to inhale asbestos. Then they put me on the *Old Crow* account. At least liquor attacked a different part of the body. Except for maybe the matzo-ball soup at *Carnegie Deli*, healthful fare didn't exist where I liked to nosh in Manhattan. But I didn't care. I was a corn flakes man. My idea of health food was *Special K*. I hated watery skim milk. Dumped sugar and ketchup on everything and ate Hershey Bars.

The roots of my sweet tooth are in my childhood and in the ravioli (pronounced *ravioleeze*) we ate on Sundays at my grandmother's house at 20 North Georgia Avenue. *Gram's* was an unforgettable three-story reddish brick building with a wide front porch and cement steps leading to the second floor. Atlantic City's Convention Hall and Boardwalk were only two blocks away. The Scarfo's lived a couple of doors down. Nicky grew up to be a celebrated mobster, now serving a life's sentence for killing practically his whole Mafia family. On the corner was *Previti's Meat Market* where my Uncle Joe was a butcher. Previti's wiped out practically a whole generation of my family's arteries. Across the street, provolone cheeses hung from ropes in the window of Griloni's Grocery. On the opposite corner was *Polestino's Drug Store,* where they kept a big jar on the counter that gave me the creeps. Inside dozens of slimy leeches clamped themselves to the sides of the glass. People bought them to suck poison out of infected sores. The thought of it made me sick.

Just around the next corner were the heavenly aromas of freshly baked Italian bread and pizza exuding from *Panerelli's Bakery*! The place had such a glorious smell you didn't mind waiting in line on Sundays after Mass at St. Michael's. None of us could resist biting off the crunchy ends of warm loaves poking out of bags we carried back to 20 North. What a fortunate family we were. We could cut through the church parking lot, where Uncle Sammy, a carpenter, had special permission from the nuns to park his orange van. Everyone knew it was the crispy bread from *Panarelli's* that made subs from *The White House* so delicious that Frank Sinatra would have them flown out to him in California. We were privileged to live so near to *The White House* and Panerelli's heavenly scent. If we cut through the churchyard, however, we brushed the darker side of life. And maybe damnation.

For across the street from St. Michael's was a den of inequity called *Frank Morati's Poolroom*! We adored the place. We put our lunch money and our souls on the line in that smoky emporium. I wasn't allowed to go near it, but I practically lived there. On Frank's four old pocket-billiard tables, I got an education in economics. I played *points* and *pill pool* for money. I could run a rack. And I learned something about public relations, even if it was only how to promote a hot game of *nine ball.*

My dad and members of his salon orchestra used to come in after playing at the *Traymore Hotel*. Because they were all still in their tuxedos, spectators would gather around them to watch what they thought was going to be a championship tournament. *But they couldn't shoot pool worth a damn,* Frank chortled, as he chewed his tobacco and spat the juice into the spittoon near the register. Frank was like a father to us. We learned a lot about gambling and women from Frank who'd explain in vivid detail what made each so worthwhile. On weekends, Frank would let a couple of us watch Lovie Dovie and the boys in the back room shoot crap. One night I saw Lovie swallow the dice in a raid. The cops took everybody's cash and let us go. I always wondered what Lovie rolled the next morning.

The characters that hung around Frank's fascinated us, especially Lovie. He got his name from the size of his penis, which he'd occasionally display proudly on the pool table as we applauded and cheered. But much more impressive was the size of his nose. It was elephantine. Bigger than Durante's. He was Cyrano with a cue stick instead of a sword. And it was especially prominent on his small, beady head. Because of it, you had to watch Lovie carefully. He'd pretend to be closely studying a shot, but he'd be moving balls around with his nose or separating a pair that was kissing. Whenever he'd lose, which was often, he'd put his hands together prayerfully, point his prodigious nose upward and implore loudly to whomever would listen: *Take this fucking curse off!*

Aunt Josie and Aunt Rita worked as a team on Sunday, sweetening the ricotta with cinnamon and sugar. Even the meat sauce was like sugar, which they spooned on slices of Italian bread to tide me and my 10 cousins over until the feast began. The hand-made ravioli were meticulously spread over the dining room table to dry before my aunts plopped them into a huge pot of boiling water. My Uncle Joe would come up the back steps carrying succulent hunks of beef, pork and sausage for the *gravy*. Like his father, he was a master meat cutter. My grandfather had the first slaughtering house in South Philadelphia. I'd often hear what an impressive funeral he had when he died from cirrhosis of the liver. His legacy were those mega meals at Nonna's, where the Imperials gathered like a herd of hungry bison. Uncle Rudy showed everybody his silver dollar, tapping the coin with his finger and mumbling unintelligibly. Gram wore her black dress and played Solitaire. Cards were the last of her senses to succumb to Alzheimer's.

Those Sunday dinners were beyond banquets. Nobody cared about cholesterol, fat or tomorrow. They ate as if there weren't tomorrows. My Aunt Louise would even eat your skin. She'd ask whoever didn't want their chicken skin to fork it over. She weighed 400 pounds! Out of 11 children, *Lena*, my mother, was the only sibling who was thin. Because of her finicky eating habits, she was regarded by her brothers and sisters as a kind of leper. They were all big and boisterous carnivores. And when they finally finished eating, they'd all line up for my Uncle Doc, who had come down from Philadelphia, to take their blood pressures. He'd do it in amazement that they were all still alive. Aunt Louise gave him the most trouble as he could hardly fit his pressure pad around her fleshy arm.

Afterward they'd adjourn to the living room for Pinochle. The Imperiales were fierce card players. *Sal! Why the hell did ya lead trump? You sittin' on your brains?* one of my uncles would boom. While they battled indoors with their clubs and hearts, my cousins and I fought outside with water pistols and grapes. We picked our ammunition off the vines in the backyard. We'd soak and splatter each other until my uncles started yelling at us to cut it out. Except Uncle Tony who went to live in Florida and lasted until his eighties, my aunts and uncles on my mother's side died in their 60s and 70s. And except for Uncle Tony and Uncle Doc, they were all overweight when they keeled over, mostly from heart attacks, diabetes, kidney failure and cancer. Meanwhile, they constantly teased my mother. An Italian American girl who wouldn't eat meat balls! It was a sacrilege. Today, Clementine is nearly 90, lives by herself and walks a couple of miles a day. Her doctor looks admiringly at her blood work-up. He wishes his looked as good.

Her diet consists of tons of frozen vegetables, lentil and chicken soup, unsweetened canned peaches, unsalted cottage cheese, raisins, prunes, bran muffins, wheat germ and bananas washed down with orange, prune and cranberry juice, plus a daily shot of Christian Brothers brandy. But the sauce at her mother's house on Sundays was something else. So thick and sweet you'd lick your fingers. And over ravioli, it was a killer dish.   Later on when I was a spin man hustling around the canyons of New York, my idea of culinary utopia was a mound of corned beef, coated with creamy Cole slaw and Russian dressing so thick you could plaster walls with it. It would be years before I would discover fat-free frozen chocolate yogurt or switch to rum and diet Coke. We didn't get serious about health until we moved our PR business to the Sunshine State.

14

Oh Yes, I've Seen It All...
New York. Washington. Palm Beach!
–Norma Shearer In Idiot's Delight

Some days, I think a more fitting name for our firm—which we moved to New York's Riviera: South Florida—would be Danny Rose Public Relations. Angela would bring in Sidney from the reception room, who'd come into my office wearing a bag over his head. I'd try to make out what he's murmuring, but his voice is muffled, so I can't make out what he's saying. Sidney is ahead of his time—way ahead. He claims his patented plastic bag can save people from dying in fires from smoke inhalation. With it you can scoop up a reservoir of air that's breathable for three minutes. Enough time to escape a smoke-filled building. He came in this morning with the guy holding a teddy bear? Don't make a big deal about it. He's the creator of "Send A Hug," a telemarketer of hugs via a toll-free number. And he's very sensitive and shy. He's waiting to hug me. And you know how healthful a hug is? If more people got them, we'd have a lot less sickness. We're interrupted when the phone rings. It's the stripper calling who was bitten by the Federal Prosecutor. *Wait a minute, Sidney, I've got to take this call.* She tells me the prosecutor bought her a $1,000 bottle of champagne.

They were in the private room talking. Honestly. Just talking. Then he tried to kiss her—strictly against the rules.

She pushed him off, but his mouth brushed against her arm and he bit down hard. The teeth marks were barely visible now, but her husband had photographed them for posterity and maybe a lawsuit. She asked me what *Inside Edition* might pay for her story? I put her on hold and called *Inside Edition*. The sound of Tibetan singing bowls is coming from Kristin's office. We hired Kristin from the *National Enquirer's Weekly World News*.

Sidney's starting to turn blue. Why me? I wondered. Why not Jack Nicholson in Chinatown? Why not take their Maltese Falcons in plastic bags to Sidney Greenstreet or Humphrey himself. *How much? Inside Edition* was offering her a tidy sum, of which we would get a third. *Sidney please get the bag off your head. You're choking. And I've got a stripper holding and a hug waiting.* I tell the stripper what *Inside Edition* is willing to pay. She accepts. The intercom rings. It's that Indian with his PILEX hemorrhoid remover. I tell him what he can do with it if he can't afford our fee. Then another call comes in. It's the MBA who invented the *invisible jump rope*. He swears it's another *pet rock*.

I shout to Lina, "Honey, I'm busy. Tell him I can't promote what I can't see. And I can't see anyone buying it. And tell Schwerter I'll have to get back to him on his Egyptian mummies. Tell him Danny Rose is busy interviewing. And cancel my 3 o'clock on the electric wand. Impotent males actually stick it up their rectum? It really jump starts an erection? How gross! I'd rather be a eunuch! Doesn't it take some of the spontaneity out of love making? It's like when you gave up everything impulsive for Lent and I asked you if we could have sex a week from Friday. And move the appointment with the DHEA hormone replacement lady. Tell her we think it's wonderful it increases breast size. But will women appreciate all that facial hair? Confirm my meeting on the radiation free breast screening."

I wonder if their laser can circumnavigate Tova's tits. Imagine orbiting those mother earths. Yes, you name it. I've heard it and seen it. . . sitting there in my office, fidgeting, preening, bragging, bellowing, bullshitting, crying, conniving and suffocating for my services which they believe will make them or their products famous or at least better known or not as bad as they're reputed to be. Yet too often they want fame by 5 o'clock and I have to negotiate for a little more time. "Honey, please come in and help Sidney get the bag off his head. And you can send in the hugger. But tell him no kissing. I mean it. NO KISSING!"

I gave up Manhattan mostly to please my Barese wife, who means more to me than I'll bet Beatrice ever meant to Dante. Besides being a classic beauty herself, mi amore Angela is my business partner and a sharp, no-nonsense bookkeeper. She knows more about what's going on financially with our business than I do. And she knows, like my father before me, I'm a little too loose with the money. But she longs for the warmer, sunnier climes of her native Italy. So one wintery gray day in Manhattan, she points her high cheekbones at me and with irresistible Italian logic gives me two powerful reasons why we should relocate to Florida. *I want to move. You can stay here and freeze by yourself!* So we migrate to that village by the sea synonymous with the rich and famous. Palm Beach. Where everyone knows everybody who's anybody from Hollywood to The White House.

We begin to feel out of sorts at soirees because we're the only ones not on intimate terms with the Sultan of Brunei, King Hussein, Ron Perlman, George Hamilton, Alexander Haig, Adnom Kashodi, Frank Sinatra, Shimon Perez and, of course, Teddy, Prince Charles and Queen Elizabeth. A well-tailored man with a European accent tells me at a cocktail party what a close friend he is of the Queen. *If I call her, the bitch is going to call me back.* Another guy says he'll let us promote one of his products, but when we mention our monthly fee, he rails: *I got $29 million in gold coins buried in Beirut. So don't talk to me about little fees.* We meet many Palm Beachers, who are affable enough, but aloof from that humdrum place—*reality*—or from anything related to earning a living. We become friendly with a Cuban-Ethel-Merman merchant named Vilda dePorro. We met Vilda at Tova's $20 million lakefront home. Vilda sells precious antiques to mega shoppers like Donald Trump and Michael Jackson. At her opulent Worth Avenue store, she serves deliciously-rich espresso to customers on her Louie the Something desk. We organized a party together for Julio Iglesias at Mar-a-Lago that included a surprise birthday cake for Marla. Behind Gucci's, across Worth Avenue from Vilda's store, our firm produced its first big event in Florida, an outdoor reception for Yoko Ono. About 700 invitees came to celebrate the opening of an exhibition of her art works. The pieces ranged from a $100,000 basket series of bronze cats with illumined eyes to a small metal box with a mirrored bottom entitled "A Box of Smiles." Open it and you see inside the schmuck who paid $6,000 for it. It does kind of make you grin. The only one not smiling is Yoko. She dreads the crowds that paw over her, gawk at her avant-garde conceptual creations and snicker at their price tags. She's heard every platitude. Every compliment for her murdered working-class-hero husband. And every hurtful, whispered insult. For her it's another *Hard Day's Night*. But the art must go on.

Haifa-born Tova is a former "Miss Israel" whose bosom erupts into the mother of all cleavage. That plus her fiery Israeli temperament swept poor Arthur Leidesdorf off his feet at an Israel Bonds dinner. It cost him millions, not for Israel, but to divorce his wife. And he proceeded to deluge Tova in wealth created by his father, Sam, who was Albert Einstein's financial advisor. His dad built Manhattan skyscrapers in partnership with the Rockefellers.

Their photographs together with those of former Presidents, Secretaries of State, potentates and movie stars who've been Tova's house guests, plus a hand-signed copy of Nixon's letter resigning the Presidency, adorn her piano, end tables and the walls of her study. A spiral staircase leads to the upstairs rooms, to which you can also get to by elevator. Tova calls me *Tomella* and is ever promising to introduce me to billionaires, including her close friend Ted Arison, owner of Carnival Cruise Lines. She calls me once every three months or so with her call waiting clicking incessantly. *Let me get rid of THEM* (click), she says impatiently as if they were bugs that needed to be stomped on. Usually I can decipher the purpose of her call, but first I have to wade through billionaires she says she's going to introduce me to. Meanwhile, there's always a phone number or a name she needs, like Joe Jack, the former president of Waste Management and a close friend of Wayne Huizenga, who I once brought to one of her parties. Joe's an investor. And Tova's always looking for people to invest in the colossal deals of her billionaire friends. And I'm sure one day I'll get to meet one of those billionaires.

The Party At Tova's

One of the key things you must do in PR is to keep the landscape moving and the scenery ever interesting for your clients. Better yet, make it exciting. Different! Introduce them to famous people. Like arranging for Rexall Sundown's chairman, Carl DeSantis, to meet Vice President Dan Quayle and spend an hour with him privately in his room at the Boca Raton Hotel & Club. I could tell Carl was impressed. And grateful. Take clients to parties at Mar-a-Lago. Introduce them to The Donald. The impression you want to make is: *Wow, our PR guy knows everybody.* Little do they know you can introduce anyone to anyone, even to people you hardly know. Who's going to mind? People appreciate it. It makes it lively. And fun. And makes the spin man look good. So this past spring I had this great idea. I asked Tova if she would host a party for our client Cellular One, now AT&T Wireless Services. They were looking for an unusual venue to hold their annual awards program and banquet. Tova's $20 million Palm Beach mansion would be an unusual venue. I told her that in return I could arrange free cellular phones and service for her and her son, Edmund. Cellular One would, of course, pay for the catering. And it would be great exposure for her mansion, which she was looking to unload. She loved the idea. And I went to Ken Manfredi, Cellular One's director of corporate accounts with it.

Ken, how'd you like your awards banquet to be a ritzy black-tie affair held at a private, lakefront mansion that will impress the hell out of everybody? And listen to this. I could get the mansion for you, Ken, for just a couple of phones.

Ken loves it. He provides the portable phones and complimentary service for Tova and Edmund. He sends formal invitations to his people and goes a patent-leather step further. He hires limousines to squire them to Tova's mansion, where a photographer would be waiting at the door to photograph their arrival. It's a brilliant plan. And everyone at Cellular One is agog with anticipation.

The day before the grand event, it drizzles in Palm Beach. I receive a call from Tova's secretary. And I can't believe what I was hearing.

"Mrs. Leidesdorf wishes to cancel the party."

"I'm sorry, I don't understand."

"Mrs. Leidesdorf wishes to cancel the affair tomorrow night due to the rain."

"No, please, she can't do that. It's too late. They're all coming. It's too late to stop them."

"Well you'd better head them off because the gate will be closed." (Click)

I call right back and ask to speak with Tova. When Tova comes on, she sounds upset.

"Tomella, I can't do it."

"Why not, Tova?"

"The rain. Tomella, it's awful. I don't want those fucking Cellular One people ruining my home. Tell Ken to go somewhere else. It's impossible. I'm so upset, Tomella. I should never have agreed. No, absolutely not. I won't have them here with this fucking rain. And no insurance. My attorneys started yelling. They want a million-dollar policy. But even if they gave me insurance, Tomella, I still don't want them. No! Tell Ken I'm sorry. The furnishings in this home are worth millions. And I don't want you to get hurt, Tomella. They'll traipse in here with their wet feet. Ruin my home. Oh, this is horrible. I can't bear to think of it. Goodbye Tomella. I'm sorry. I'm so upset!"

I swallow hard. I can imagine how Ken is going to receive this news. Ken is a short Brooklyn guy with an even shorter temper. He's built like Mike Tyson. And is about as mean if you cross him. He doesn't mince words about where you stand with him. And if you tick him off too much, you might not be standing very long. I call Tova back and try to plead with her, but it's like pleading with an Israeli tank after a Palestinian raid. Then I call Ken.

"She what?"

"That's right, Ken, she's calling off the party."

"She can't do that. She promised."

"It's her house, Ken."

"You tell that bitch if her gate's not open for my people I'm going to fucking drown her in her own fucking swimming pool!"

"Ken, maybe we can find another place. I could call some fancy restaurants."

"No, you tell her if I get there and that gate's not open, she'd better call out the National Guard." (Click)

By now I hate the PR business. Why didn't I go into something normal? Sane? I call Tova back. *No no no no. And that's final.* I call Ken back. *I'll kill her. I swear I'll kill her.* I ask Ken to provide her with a certificate of an indemnification for any damage that might be caused. He says it's too late. He could never get Cellular One's attorneys to do it in time. It's Friday. The party is tomorrow night. I tell him to dummy one up. Put it on Cellular One stationary and fax it to her. I call Tova and assure her she would be covered.

Nothing was going to happen. The 72 Cellular One people will be on their best behavior. The rain has stopped. It would be dry by tomorrow night. And Ken knows some very rich people who might be interested in buying your home. Cellular One is a powerful company with terrific contacts. Tova listens. I keep talking, promising, assuring. *Okay we'll see tomorrow night how the weather is.*

The next night Cellular One's limousines pull up Tova's oak tree-lined driveway, past her authentic Chinese Garden and swing around her water fountain to the front door where our photographer waits in his tuxedo. It's a crystal clear evening. There's hardly a trace of the previous day's rain. Tova is positively radiant. She squeals with delight as she greets Ken. They embrace. They smooch the air around each other's cheeks. *Oh you look so handsome, my Kennie. This is going to be a wonderful party. Come. My home is yours, my darling. Please. Please. I want you to meet a few of my friends. I hope you don't mind I invited them to your party.* Ken chuckles. *Of course not, Tova, it's your home,* he says graciously. The party is a huge success. The Cellular One people can't stop talking about it for weeks. Tova escapes drowning in her swimming pool. Ken dodges a humiliating, mortifying bullet. And we hold on to the Cellular One account. But it was a damn close high-tension wireless call.

15

We Kept Running Into Her Emeralds

When we first arrived in Palm Beach we met many wealthy individuals like Tova. We shake the richest hands, but none of it rubs off. We meet moguls and horse breeders, coke-sniffing Indy car racers and car dealers who had become auto barons and then Broadway producers. We bow to little emperors from Japan and nod to aristocrats like the Baroness von Something. We keep running into her emeralds, which are the size of ping-pong balls surrounding her majestic throat. And we keep seeing the same face lifts and diamonds we had seen the night before at Collette's, L'Europe or at the perennial charity galas at the Breakers. We attend polo matches, art openings and concerts at Flagler Hall. Have our pictures published in the *Shiny Sheet* and *Society East* posing with Sophia Loren and Vic Damone. But we never seem to run into a client, or even a prospect. The people with whom we were mingling have everything they want or need. We realize the business center of gravity isn't Palm Beach. That's the place for people who have it made. The people still trying to make it were further south. So we open an office an easy 20-minute commute to Boca Raton, an entrepreneurial frontier of cheeky stockbrokers and walled-cities containing the nouveau riche. I started to feel we were on target. We had traded the mean streets of Manhattan for *La Dolce Vita*. Our first client was a $100 million private company called Tasco, which distributed binoculars made in the Far East. We got *FORBES* to come down to do a story on the owners, George and Sheryl Rosenfield. The angle is a father and daughter managing a successful company so well together. While he's still at the helm in his 70s, Sheryl is breathing softly down his back, being next in the line of succession since her brother had opted out of the family business to become a doctor.

The day the reporter arrives, they get into this horrendous argument. It ends with George ordering his daughter out of the building. The story takes an abrupt turn, off a cliff. And us with it. I relate this to clients who think we can work miracles and control the press. Sure we can get their attention. Even put on a positive spin. But that's about it.

Truth has a way of breaking in; robbing you of your dignity sometimes. So it's best to embrace it. Go with it. Eventually the father and daughter made up, but they never forgave us for the embarrassing story that ran in *FORBES* about the pitfalls of family-run businesses. Eventually we attracted more stable, even Ma 'n Apple Pie Clients such as AT&T Wireless Services. Ironically, AT&T was the first client I landed when I departed NBC back in the early 1980s. At that time Ma Bell was still the mighty behemoth of telecommunications. It was still all in one piece, but about to be broken apart into giant pieces. Rewind to 1981. The scene is a table cloth restaurant near Bedminster, New Jersey.

16

It's Silverman Calling...On AT&T.

Igot my piece of Ma Bell over a momentous lunch one mild spring day in New Jersey. As far as I was concerned, it was the mother of all lunches. Herb Lennon, then Director of PR, and his boss, a Senior VP of Advertising had read my swan song article in *TV GUIDE*, which mentioned that I had started my own PR firm, TransMedia Consultants, Inc. in New York City. They invited me to lunch and took me to a fancy restaurant near Bedminister, New Jersey, the home of the AT&T Long Distance network, the telecommunications nerve center of the world. They asked me a lot of questions about the inner workings of a TV network. And since I had been the right hand man to NBC's famed CEO, they asked me a lot of questions about Fred. The one and only Fred Silverman, about whom I had just written this article for *TV GUIDE*.

Excitedly, my wife had cupped the telephone. Her eyes were bulging. "It's Silverman," she whispered. Months earlier, Fred Silverman, ABC's programming wizard, had defected to become president of NBC. It was 1978 and I was still at ABC where I had known Fred well. Now he was on the phone—perhaps with a job offer?

My wife dashed over to turn the TV to NBC. What if the Wunderkind wanted to know what I was watching? (Why, *Another World,* Fred. What else would I be doing at home on vacation?) But he didn't want to know what I was watching; he wanted to see me. The next day I hurried over to the sixth floor of the then-RCA Building, where there really is Another World—the office of the president. Silverman's name was making headlines. He was magic. That's why, when he did offer me a job, I jumped.

Fred wanted me to help him with his speeches and correspondence and represent him at meetings. Overnight I zoomed up the ranks to Somebodyhood in television. Suddenly I was a Vice President and Assistant to the President of NBC. I can't tell you how proud I was. Proud as a you-know-what.

That was less than three years ago. A few months ago I jumped again—or rather I was pushed—into that long line of battle-weary VPs who no longer work for NBC. The official reason was that I was the victim of a budget cut. Yes, Virginia, I was pink-slipped. Am I sore at anybody? No, not even at Sheriff Lobo.

Fred Silverman might not have been the easiest guy to work for, but I'll miss his disarming qualities. At least with Fred you knew where you stood. If he thinks you're funny, he'll practically roll out of his chair laughing. If you're a lummox, one of his favorite terms of non-endearment—look out. Fred's not above speaking his mind to anybody. "Don't call me 'Freddie'," he admonished a reporter once, "'Freddie' is what you call a cocker spaniel."

If he likes you, he'll give you the egg roll off his plate. In 1978, however, I found him surrounded by more than egg rolls. His coterie of execs were up to their pinstripes in a chop suey of deals. With cigarette smoke wafting in his face, Fred pored over program-development reports as thick as Manhattan phone books and about as interesting. But he was Fred—always ebullient and optimistic. "I'm still optimistic about the future" might well be his epitaph. So, with glee, I jumped into that chop suey beside him.

My first assignment was to produce a blizzard. In August, Fred asked me to write a little promotional show that could be shown by closed-circuit TV to NBC's affiliate stations. It was supposed to get them excited about our '78 midseason schedule. So I created *Winter In Burbank*, starring Paul Klein, then NBC's head of programming, with Fred putting in a cameo appearance. My script called for mountainous snowbanks, howling wind machines and barking huskies.

Klein described our "sizzling" schedule as he trudged through the snow, perspiring in his parka. Too bad the public didn't get a chance to see the droll Mr. Klein; he was never funnier. Unfortunately, the comedies he talked about weren't half as funny. Fred thought the whole production "dazzling" until he got the bill.

I remember the shows that had their premieres during Fred's first season at NBC. I wondered how they could compete with the arsenal he himself had built when he was at CBS and ABC. Our big gun was *The Waverly Wonders*. It was to be our secret weapon. As it turned out, the secret was that it was a comedy. It starred Joe Namath, and all I can tell you is that it wasn't one of his Brut days.

There followed a succession of comedies that proved witless and hitless. The worse these shows got, it seemed, the louder their laugh tracks roared. This would only infuriate Fred. "Who are they kidding? Send it back!" he'd rail, stomping out of a screening room and slamming the door on the rest of us. When he screened *Different Strokes*, however, his spirits soared. Fred knew what a comedy was. He knew *The Mary Tyler Moore Show, Maude* and *M*A*S*H*; he knew *The Love Boat, Laverne & Shirley* and *Soap*. He'd played a major role in putting all of them on the air. But his own successful past was his own toughest adversary.

When George Schlatter, who had clicked big before as the producer of *Laugh-In*, walked in with a pilot called *Real People*, Fred was ecstatic. Sure enough, *Real People* started a trend that's still going strong.

Then Schlatter came up with a creation that nearly started World War III. *Speak Up America* was despised by everyone. Even our affiliates howled that it was strident, shallow, anti-Establishment. But Fred said wait, give it a chance. Was this not, after all, a Schlatter production?

And hadn't Fred, back when we were both at ABC, begged for another controversial new show to be given a chance? That was how *Soap* began. But *Speak Up America* was no *Soap*.

One of the best pilots I saw at NBC was *A Man Called Sloane*, a James Bond-type adventure. And one of the worst nights I spent at NBC occurred shortly after Fred had decided the good-looking guy playing Sloane was all wrong for the part. Never mind that the star had elaborate stunts and special effects and breathtaking scenery backing him up. It's not razzle-dazzle that holds audiences, Fred had explained. It's stories, characters, actors. So the order had gone out to find a new Sloane and now, here we were, the night before our new schedule was to be announced, and we still hadn't come up with a replacement. Fred kept shaking his head. How could something like this have happened? Two senior executives in the room with us also shook their heads and left NBC shortly thereafter.

Robert Conrad eventually took over as Sloane, but the series flopped anyway, ending the way it began, with too many gimmicks. The Wunderkind was fallible, after all. Once he scolded an executive for scheduling a certain promotional spot in the middle of a Clint Eastwood movie. The promo was for a comedy that appealed to kids, and we all knew from research that the movie appealed to older males.

> "I never heard of such a dumb thing in my life!" Silverman kept snarling as the guy sat in his office, glum-faced, wondering who on his staff had fouled up. After taking the heat for several minutes, he and another executive left Fred's office.
>
> "I didn't want to say anything in there," the other exec said. "But you know who put that promo there?"
>
> "Who?"
>
> "He did."

It's not hard to understand how Fred could make such a mistake; at times it seemed as though he never slept. Once he asked an executive why the late-night Tomorrow show didn't carry any promotional spots for the next morning's *Today Show*.

"Fred, how many people watch both shows?" the executive asked rhetorically.

"I do," Fred answered.

He got the worst breaks imaginable, but the killer was the boycott of the Summer Olympics—the network's big hope for a ratings turnaround. Around the time the Soviets invaded Afghanistan, Fred started examining his skin. "I expect to wake up one day and find warts," he told me. More recently he joked with Hollywood producers that "If J.R. had been on NBC and somebody took a shot at him, they would have missed."

The black humor wasn't far from the truth. Remember a 1979 series called *Sweepstakes*? It seemed sure-fire—an escapist show about people who could win up to a million dollars in a state lottery, Shades of *The Millionaire*. But *Sweepstakes* bombed in the ratings. Viewers felt that the wrong characters in the show were winning the lottery. Talk about not being able to pick a winner.

All in all I have to say I like Fred Silverman, even if talking to him sometimes was like talking to a spectator at a tennis match. He had three screens to the right of his desk. He'd look at you, then at the screens, then back at you, then at the screens.

But I know what he's been through trying to keep those screens filled. The disappointments. Those noble experiments to make innovative shows work: *Lifeline, Skag, United States*, Yes, even David Letterman in daytime.

It was a challenge to work for this indefatigable optimist and I don't regret a minute of it. That's why I mean it when I say . . . Good luck, Fred.

I was still talking about Silverman at the lunch when I was interrupted and asked a question that made the olives shake in my Martini. *What fee would you charge to represent us?*

Having just fallen from that precipice known as NBC . . . and now without office, secretary, clients or even prospects . . . having surrendered my most treasured asset, my NBC credit card, and been evicted from 30 Rock . . . and to my children's greatest dismay, having forfeited an unlimited supply of VIP passes to the hottest show in town, *Saturday Night Live*, and now having reached the most humiliating stage of my life—waiting for my first unemployment check . . . I took a long sip of my dry Martini and blurted out six figures.

Okay, the top guy said, but could I start right away booking Charley Brown on *The Today Show* and *CBS Morning*? *Sure*, I said managing somehow not to stammer. *Good, then we'll send you over a contract on Monday.* That night I told Angela and the kids that we were going to sell our Long Island home, move into the city and open an office. We had the largest client in the world on a full-year contract. AT&T would renew that wonderful contract four wonderful times, while we added Drexel Burnham Lambert, Met Life and The City of New York. For the latter we created a PSA campaign pairing Mayor Koch and Mr. T as a dynamic duo who'd fight discrimination in city housing wherever they found it. It won us the Emmy Award of PR, a Bronze Anvil from the Public Relations Society of America. And I got Charley Brown, the AT&T Chairman, all of the media bookings he wanted. And then some!

Fast forward to our Boca Raton office and allow me to introduce you to a few of the clients who've come after AT&T.

17

Heil C!

The square-jawed, broad-shouldered stocky fella in the corner is Dr. Matthias Rath, an M.D. from Germany. He's sulking because the medical community won't give him a standing ovation. And wearing his customary brown shirt and double-breasted brown suit, he looks guilty sitting there picking lint off his pants. He was once the chief lieutenant to Vitamin C Rights Marshall Linus Pauling. And if he ever got to be a fuhrer, this protegé of the late Pauling probably would require us all to take thousands of milligrams of Vitamin C daily or be sent to a nutritional re-education camp. The reason? He believes devoutly in a Master Nutrient that can conquer the world . . . of heart disease. You almost want to click your heels and say "Heil C" to this Germanic zealot who has sworn obedience to an omnipotent nutrient. He has little patience with non-believers. He carries an X-ray showing that not a single spec of calcium dares deposit itself on his Aryan arteries. And he carries dark sunglasses, which I'm sure with all of the Vitamin C in his system, he wears when he urinates. Because he's not licensed in the U.S., you don't have to call him *doctor*. But he holds the first patent ever given for the reversal of heart disease using Vitamin C. And he is the author of *Why Animals Don't Get Heart Attacks*. It presents convincing evidence that animals avoid the dangers of clogged arteries because their bodies manufacture high levels of certain key vitamins like Vitamin C. Humans can't do this anymore.

As if that's not bad enough, the stress hormone adrenaline uses up our body's limited supply. This is why he exhorts everyone to take daily supplements. The problem with Rath is not his theory, but his temperament. You almost want to spell his surname with a "W" since he's constantly mad at the medical community for not taking him more seriously. He believes pharmaceutical companies snub him because they can't patent vitamins. If they can't turn an inexpensive natural substance into a pricey synthetic alternative—and have exclusive rights to market it—they won't do the research. Pharmaceutical companies are in business to make money, not save the world. And that's precisely the thinking that makes Rath so wrathful. The more he dwells on it, the more fanatical he becomes.

Like most saviors, Rath is a demagogic-type who has an exaggerated sense of his own importance. He charged that Rexall was understating sales of his Vitamin C formulations and therefore not paying him enough royalties. The company offered to show him the sales figures, but instead of examining figures, he preferred making charges. Rath's tinderbox ego made him difficult to deal with. Then he tried a kind of nutritional coup d'etat. Rexall Showcase International had to dump him as a consultant after he tried to Pied Piper away their independent distributors. Rath is bitter about his dismissal, so much so that the Circuit Court in Palm Beach County had to shut him up. It granted Rexall's request for a Temporary Restraining Order. Rath's the only guy I ever met who can put an acerbic spin on ascorbic acid, which makes him hard to stomach.

The day before the injunction was granted, Rath came to Florida to stir up trouble on Rexall's home turf. Bent on embarrassing the company, and maybe forcing a settlement, he sent out a news tip to all of the media in South Florida announcing a news conference at which he was going to blast our client one more time.

Rexall called an emergency PR meeting in Carl DeSantis' office. There were investment bankers in the boardroom down the hall putting together a major new stock offering. Bad press was the last thing they needed at this moment. As usual I let everyone speak first. The consensus was to attack with a preemptive strike. Everyone was fed up with Rath's absurd allegations and wanted to fight back. The company would issue a release refuting every one of his ridiculous charges. And a Rexall representative would go to Rath's news conference to give the company's side. And then they all looked at me, their spin man, for concurrence. I shook my head. *No that would be playing right into his hands*, I said. *You've got to treat Rath as a minor annoyance. Get into the ring with him and you make him a much bigger story. Besides that I don't think the press will show up at his news conference.* I saw his amateurish news tip and knew he had a reputation for grandstand plays like this. *The Press will see him for what he is, a disgruntled former contractor with an axe to grind.* They agreed to play it my way. But I better be right.

Rath held his news conference later that afternoon. Only one person showed up. It was Glen Calder. If Rath is still waiting for Glen's story to appear, it's going to be quite a while since Glen works for us. He is one of our account executives. And Glen knows how to look and sound like a reporter. His father is Iain Calder, President of *The National Enquirer*. We sent Glen to take notes. And assuming he was press, Rath gave him a 45-minute one-on-one presentation. Glen dutifully wrote down everything Rath told him and then went straightaway to Rexall's attorneys for debriefing. The injunction hearing was scheduled the next day and his notes would be enormously helpful. I called Damon DeSantis, the President of Rexall Showcase International, the company's direct sales subsidiary, in his car. When I told him the only *reporter* who showed up was our Glen, Damon laughed so hard I was worried his car might leave the road. *Call Carl and Chris. They'll get a kick out of it*, he said still cackling. *I love it*, Carl said. By this time I couldn't stop laughing myself. Chris Nast, Rexall's President, said *All right, Tom, now don't get cocky on us.* He was right. The spin man must be cool.

18

Keeping America Healthy, He Made A Fortune

The vitamin supplier Rexall Sundown was a much better example of a family business than Tasco. CEO Carl DeSantis started the business 18 years ago in the bedroom of his house, where he and his wife Sylvia slapped labels on bottles, which they sold mail order through the *National Enquirer*. Because they didn't have a machine to do it for them, they had to count the number of vitamins they put into bottles by hand. Carl told me once that back in those days, *If a bottle said 100 tablets, we always put in a few extra to make sure there was at least a hundred. We thought it's better to go over than under.* Adhering to that philosophy, DeSantis built a company known for giving consumers more than they paid for. Instead of a family business, he likens it to *a business with a family in it.* More than 20 years ago, Carl saw the vitamin craze coming. And his business grew profitable.

In 1985 he shrewdly bought one of the most respected names in health care—*Rexall*, of corner drugstore fame, and his business took off. He snapped up the ninety-year-old *Rexall* name in a liquidation sale at a bargain and coupled it with *Sundown*, the name he had dreamed up for a low cost suntan lotion he created while managing a drug store in North Miami Beach. *Rexall* was not his first bonanza deal.

When he was 14 years old, he used $12 he had saved up selling newspapers on street corners in Miami and bought an aviary of parakeets. Eight months later he sold the business for $250.

In 1993, Carl took his company public and we played a supporting role in helping its stock take off into the stratosphere. In three years, it increased over 600%. Maybe we were too good in getting Carl and his company so much press, including appearances on CNBC and the *Nightly Business Report* and favorable articles in *The Wall Street Journal* and *Investor's Business Daily* because in October 1996, *Barrons* magazine said Rexall Sundown was one of the most overvalued stocks in the country. Carl loved the terse response I wrote:

Having achieved leadership in the rapidly growing nutritional supplement industry, and being so well positioned for dramatic expansion, it's not surprising to us that the investment community—seeing such a bright future for our company—has placed a high value on our stock.

Three days later Carl filed a registration with the Securities Exchange Commission for an offering to sell four million more shares of stock worth about $120 million, including 2 million owned by the DeSantis family.

The way Carl would bubble over some of my ideas, it reminded me of another impulsive wunderkind I worked for, Fred Silverman at NBC. *You rascal you, I love it*, Carl chortled one day when I showed him a Sundown vitamin jar I had made into a bright-orange rocket. I wanted to send it out to trade press to symbolize the record speed with which Sundown had just hit the market with a new Selenium product. Sundown had it formulated, labeled and had ready for shipping within 48 hours of a national news report that a major study had found the mineral had slashed cancer death rates in subjects.

What President Bush once called *the vision thing*, Carl had it big time. But like many successful entrepreneurs, he wasn't born farsighted. He had to learn it. Once Carl came close to not making a position on his high school football team. He had thrown a pass that had fallen short of the marker it needed to reach for him to make the team. On a second try, he aimed at the fence well beyond the marker and the ball sailed past where it had to reach. *I learned from that experience that people set their own boundaries in life.*

19

In All The PR Firms In All The Towns In The World, She Has To Walk Into Mine!

You never know who's going to walk in the door next. Get a whiff of that Jasmin? That's Mrs. Tepperman. She comes in wearing a blue silk dress that matches her sky blue eyes. She comes into my office unannounced, closes my door and sits down. *Can this be strictly confidential?* I nod. *Do you know who I am?* I squint wishing I could light a cigarette, but I gave up smoking 20 years ago. *I'm Denese Tepperman.* Wham! The headlines come back. Big ones! Her husband Fred was billionaire Ron Perelman's chief financial guy. Fred Tepperman had engineered the Revlon buy out and other colossal deals that made Perelman the wealthiest man in America. Perelman had to be to afford his hefty divorces settlements, like the $80 million he coughed up to shed wife #2, TV gossip Claudia Cohen. And now his third marriage was like last week's mascara—gone. The cosmetics heir had secretly filed for divorce from wife # 3, Patricia Duff, after 21 months.

Their quarreling erupted into a doozy during the Chicago Democratic Convention. And the split was sealed during a makeup attempt at Perelman's Long Island estate when after he had her searched he discovered she was wearing a concealed tape recorder. Now Fred had gone after Perelman and also had gotten his piece of him. A lawsuit Fred had brought against his former employer for firing him ended in a whopping settlement. Perelman had fired Fred claiming he had missed too much work while staying home caring for his terminally ill wife. The settlement cost Perelman millions and had made him look pretty damn callous toward poor Fred, who was only doing his duty. But was he? Denese told me otherwise. Fred had stayed at home to care for her. She was his dying wife's nurse. And I could see why he cared for her. Denese was slim, attractive and intense. Before his former wife died, Fred got a Dominican divorce, married Denese and they moved into a $2 million home he bought for her in Boca Raton. *Now he's divorcing me and I want it in the papers. Can you do that for me, Tom? Sure,* I said. (Sam is playing *As Time Goes By* on the Tibetan Singing Bowls.) She drops her card on my desk. *That's my beeper number on the back.* She stops at the door and smiles. *Not a big story, Tom. Just little ones in the New York Times and the New York Post. Sure,* I nodded as Rick would do in *Casablanca* if confronted with such a request by a beautiful woman. *I'll get you those exit visas. Don't worry your pretty head. Leave it up to me. From now on, kid, let me do the thinking for both of us.* Cut! Print!

We're All Spinners At Heart. And Jerry Has Come To Save Us!

Wave to our most electric-eclectic client, Dr. Jerry Jacobson. He's a walking low-level energy field who's shaking up the medical community with his preaching that he can control structure and functioning of human tissue by applying the laws of physics. He has created a device called *The Jacobson Resonator*. This ashen-faced, retired oral surgeon is the ultimate spin man. He sermonizes that all biological systems comprise tiny spinning magnets or atoms—sub atomic particles—protons and electrons. And if we can influence how a biological particle vibrates or how aggregations of particles vibrate, we can influence various biological functions. Ergo *The Jacobson Resonator*. It shoots electromagnetic fields through biological systems, mechanically vibrating such targets as genes, enzymes, neuro-transmitters and hormones. And since micro constituents can communicate and talk sense into each other through the language of frequency, they can re-orient their atomic crystal structure, thereby introducing order and coherence in molecules and biological systems who can't otherwise *bewave* themselves. Thus, by restoring the coherent domain on which all biology is based, The Jacobson's Resonator can correct disorders.

When not spinning his theories, Jacobson—a self-proclaimed genius with an IQ of 200—is creating oil paintings and playing the sax. His droopy eyelids and Roman-Forum haircut belie a glowing-hot gray matter, whose reach often exceeds his scientific grasp. He once claimed he had a cure for AIDS. "Do you believe that I have the cure for AIDS?" he asked a child with AIDS at a news conference at his Jupiter condo. The Florida teenager nodded that she did believe. For years, Jerry has committed himself to curing her. He played the saxophone on CBS' 1995 documentary *Angelie's Secret*, which traced the then-bubbly fifth-grader's joys and disappointments the year she told her classmates she had AIDS. Today, Jerry has reinvented himself. He doesn't claim to have a "cure" anymore, at least publicly. Reluctantly, he uses the more scientifically correct word—*treatment*. And he now focuses on less headline-grabbing diseases, such as Parkinson's and pain. And on our recommendation, he has given up on mainstream-medicine bashing.

Jacobson has become a muted version of his admittedly "eccentric" self. Thanks to U.S. Senate Majority Leader Trent Lott of Mississippi, Jerry's on the verge of landing a deal involving NASA. Lott's office put in a good word for his invention that uses extremely weak electromagnetic fields to reduce pain and treat neurological disorders such as Parkinson's disease, cancer and the "A" word. If the deal goes through—and NASA officials believe it has a very good chance—Jerry's machine would be built at NASA's Stennis Space Center and tested at the University of Mississippi. We describe Jerry's machine as capable of treating diseases usually treated with drugs, such as AZT for AIDS patients or dopamine-replenishing drugs for people suffering from Parkinson's disease. Jacobson's theory, if proved, would eliminate the need for such treatments as radiation and chemotherapy—and their side effects. That's what makes it so fantastic to many in scientific circles. And so appealing to victims like Angelie. We were just in the early stages of implementing a campaign of promoting Jacobson's "electromagnetic machine" to health and business editors around the world when we receive a letter from his agent terminating our services. It had been nearly two whole months and we still hadn't put him on the cover of any magazines. It was fine with me as I have an instant dislike for anyone who rejects me. Two months later, however, after having tried other publicity firms, Jacobson sends a repentant representative to see us. He promises that Jerry will be more patient and cooperative if we would please take him back as a client. We agreed and resumed spinning Jerry's molecules again on national media.

Next there's pharmacologist Jim Jamison and his marketing sidekick Mike Wallerstein. They've created *The Male Clinic*, a consortium of doctors dedicated to helping impotent men fuck again. We joke about grouping it with our two other medical institutions. If you say them real fast: *Jackson Memorial Medical Center . . . Strang-Cornell Medical Center . . . The Male Clinic*. It sounds like *Mayo Clinic*. But The *Male Clinic* is no *Mayo Clinic*. And the joke going around our office is that it has an *E-male address*: VIRILITY.COME. The Male Clinic is a fractional franchise targeting GP's and other doctors. They pay a monthly fee to belong to it, to be included as a member physician in its advertising and have the exclusive rights to a four-step Male Clinic program. It involves: 1) Virility Intensity Training; 2) An all-natural topical ointment used as an erection booster (one of my irreverent staffers says it's many times more effective when applied by Christie Brinkley); 3) Oral chelation to cleanse the arterial system and 4) Male testosterone replacement.

All my life I've been selling phoney goods to people of meager intelligence and great faith.
–*Idiot's Delight*

That coven in the corner are Latoya Jackson, Bridget Nielsen, Mother Love, Elizabeth Sandford from *The Jeffersons*, and the Psychic Twins. They belong to the Zodiac Group. No need to introduce you. They know who you are and what's going to happen to you. Zodiac runs one of the country's largest psychic hot lines, those 900 numbers wishful ninnies call every day to find out their future. It's a cash cow we're wishing to take public. Recognize Dick & Kari Clark? Of course you do. Dick's face is an icon. America's perennial teenager is a spokesperson for vitamin seller Rexall Sundown, Inc., one of our more conservative clients, but not too conservative to supply 80 percent of the shark cartilage supplements sold in America. Their Sundown line is America's #1 broadline category vitamin sold in Wal-Mart, K-mart, Thrifty Payless and at other retail outlets across the country. But one Sundown product, *Dick Clark's Formula For Life* multi vitamin was never a big hit. But Clark was bookable. And he liked promoting Rexall. He'd recall in TV interviews how his mom kept vitamins in the refrigerator when he was a kid. And he's been taking *Sundown* for years, or is it *centuries*. His energy truly amazes us on media tours. He is a tireless campaigner. Are vitamins his source of energy? Or the catnaps in limousines. Hold it. How did she get into this tableau? You're right, that's Elke. We promoted her public television series *Painting With Elke Sommer*. And next to her is Kathryn Crosby. I went on the road to Toronto with Kathryn promoting her big blue coffee table book "My Life With Bing." Afterward, she wrote me: *Working with you is a joy. So let's hope that our 'Road to ...' is a long one.* It was. And a delightful one.

The "Spin Baby" reading a press release, no doubt.

The circa six-year-old "Spin Boy" sans brief-case. . . drumming-up clients in Atlantic City.

Tom Madden's beloved father, the Gypsy violinist/orchestra leader. Concert violinist with the Cleveland Symphony.

One of Madden's first jobs as a reporter with the *Philadelphia Inquirer* covering the financial collapse of the Penn Central Railroad.

The author at a taping of the TV series pilot he produced called *I Dream of Money* starring Dan Dorfman.

Madden co-hosted his own TV Show, *Video Newscasting Network*, which was a behind-the-scenes look at the television business.

Kathryn Crosby receives 16 keys to Texas City. Madden handled all publicity.

Look who's calling. Author getting some glamorous mileage for
AT&T Wireless Services with Elke Sommer.

Madden with Dan Quayle.

Angela Madden and Gina
Lollibrigida.

Madden and the
ever youthful icon,
Dick Clark.

NBC Today Show weatherman Willard Scott tastes chicken soup during the mock battle Madden created between grandmothers and the makers of Contact as each side claimed theirs was the preferred cold remedy.

Madden helped Princess Yasmin Aga Khan promote the first Rita Hayworth Gala at the Pierre Hotel. It raised over one million dollars for the Alzheimer's Foundation.

20

Dreaming Of Kathryn Crosby And A White Christmas

These two actresses couldn't be any more different or adorable or more wonderful to be with. Elke is earthy, artistic and fun. Kathryn reserved, cerebral and fun. Elke could inspire, Kathryn could be persuasive. My wife and I were crazy about both of them. Kathryn used to stay with us up in our 23rd-floor apartment at Madison Green off Broadway at 22nd Street whenever she came to Manhattan. She'd plop her feet up on our coffee table, get herself all snugly in my wife's terry bathrobe and lick spoonfuls of Nutella Italian chocolate from the jar. The next day we'd go out hunting titans of industry whom we hit up for sponsorships of foursomes to play in her new golf tournament with celebrities like Chicago Bears ex-coach Mike Ditka and the legend himself, Bob Hope. In a peak of anger at the PGA, she moved *The Crosby* from Pebble Beach to Bermuda Run, North Carolina. She charged that the PGA had turned Bing's tournament into big business that was benefitting professional golfers much more than charity.

Raising money for a good cause while putting and chipping around a golf course had been the original idea behind Bing's *Clambake* and tournament. The idea was to help disadvantaged kids, not over privileged athletes. Now under AT&T's sponsorship, the nationally-televised tournament was casting an even bigger spotlight on the pros. Much more hurtful, it was shutting Kathryn out, diminishing her role, and the most cutting of all, it was luring her son Nathaniel into the enemy's sandtrap. I tried to bring about a truce by going to AT&T, but Kathryn felt the PGA had gone too far. It had driven a wedge between her and her son, and that was enough for her! So she packed up the Crosby name and brought it East. In place of a PRO-AM, she dropped Bing's name onto a Celebrity-AM and called it *The Bing Crosby National Championship Golf Tournament.*

With a bright new field of celebrities and corporate amateurs teeing off, the tournament once again began to fulfill the original goal of raising millions of dollars for charity. And once again Kathryn was its star. Kathryn was a trooper. She'd do just about anything we asked, within reason. She'd stride out to the pitcher's mound to address thousands of Toronto BlueJays fans. She even drove golf balls at the Statue of Liberty from a roof in Brooklyn. We were promoting a roof at the time. It was a flat roof on a news-newsprint warehouse, a couple of football fields long on the waterfront directly across from Lady Liberty. We produced a full-color brochure that pictured it as a VIP vantage for watching the Tall Ships gather in New York Harbor for the Lady's 100th birthday celebration. Kathryn was a sport about it. She did it just for us and the photographers.

Once in Rosenberg, Texas, near where her daddy was a sheriff, I got 16 mayors to present Kathryn with keys to their cities at the annual Czech Fest where she was an honored guest and kolache judge. Under the weight of all those keys suspended from ribbons around her neck, she could hardly raise her head. That's not to say she didn't have a head of her own, plus a 7-iron will when she wanted something, like when she corralled Bing after interviewing him for her college news-paper. Kathryn was a Texas gal used to roping whatever steers she set her sights on. Her sights were now on raising funds for her new tournament. She'd captivate and charm, then brand her prey with that disarming smile that still glowed like embers in the minds of millions of aging Crosby fans . . . flickering images of those marvelous finales of *Bing Crosby Family Christmas Specials* . . . of a glowing Kathryn . . .their sweet children swaying beside them, Bing bellowing Irving Berlin's immortal "White Christmas."

People would give her double-takes and stares in elevators, restaurants or on street corners when she went bike riding. She'd click on their long dormant memory files, bringing up heartwarming, fuzzy scenes from the past. Her holiday eyes would brighten and once again she'd beam that yuletide smile and say: *Hello, I'm Kathryn Crosby.* When not at her ranch in Genoa, Nevada, Kathryn ensconces herself at her stately mansion in Hillsborough, an exclusive suburb outside of San Francisco. She sits on the floor of her bedroom, notes spread out, writing the sequel to her book. A short distance away is Burlingame, home of Coit Carpet and Drapery Cleaners. I had met Kathryn through Coit on one of the cleanest carpets any hotel ever had. Coit was convening its cleaners from around the world at the Bahia Mar Hotel and Yachting Center in Fort Lauderdale. The property then belonged to the real estate division of Drexel Burnham Lambert, a high-flying client of ours that would later crash land.

Kathryn was there as Coit's spokesperson. One day I happened to be visiting the property when I noticed black hoses protruding from all orifices of the building as if a giant octopus had been locked up inside and was searching for a way out with its tentacles. But it was a massive extemporaneous cleaning job underway. And cleaners were cheering fellow cleaners doing the job. The Coit people were ticked off that the carpet in the hotel wasn't up to their high standards. When they learned that a competitor had the cleaning contract, they volunteered to clean it themselves at no charge. Kathryn and Lou Kearn, Coit's founder and CEO, were looking on as hundreds of Coit employees applauded virtuoso vacuuming of the entranceway to the ballroom. I walked up to Kearn and Kathryn and asked if they'd like to me to generate some publicity for them. They said *yes* and hired me on the spot. And I hired C.C. Goldwater, the famed Senator's granddaughter, to handle the account. At the time, she was dating Prince Albert of Monaco and I had dreams of landing the Monte Carlo account, but we rolled a seven when C.C. moved back to Arizona and married somebody else.

The program we developed for Kathryn was a simple one. We would book her on talk shows. She'd talk a little carpet cleaning, but mostly about her life with Bing. Coit bought thousands of her books, which were sold or given away free to Coit customers across the U.S. and Canada and in England where Coit held the Royal Warrant, entitling Lou's company to be the official cleaner of the Queen's drapes. At last count, Kathryn had unloaded over a 100,000 copies of her autobiography. As always, she was glad to see us whenever we were in San Francisco. The last time we saw her was a few years ago. As usual, she served us tea in her sitting room where an original Renoir graces the wall and Remingtons rise dramatically from mahogany tables. She was on her way to Russia to appear in *Uncle Vanya*. No, she had no time to be a spokesperson for one of our clients, but she appreciated the offer.

She had roped a Russian steer this time and already had memorized her part, in Russian no less. After that she was going on the road in a new production of *State Fair*. Her father, a retired Texas sheriff, was staying with her. We reminisced some past experiences, wished her a broken leg and went off to visit Larry Linderman. He had just interviewed Elke for *Playboy,* but Hugh Heffner killed the story after he saw the pictures of her at Las Hadas.

While Kathryn was classy and whimsical, I have to say Elke was more exciting. Being a male, I was maybe a tad crazier about her than my wife was. She ran on a fast track, literally.

Elke was hosting a syndicated show called *The Exciting World of Speed and Beauty.* She loved speed and was a daredevil who had driven dragsters, jet cars and had parachuted out of a plane. She had a mantle full of racing trophies won at European tracks. We recruited her to help us to promote Indy racing car driver Scott Brayton. We arranged for her to be the celebrity starter of *The Long Beach Gran Prix* one year, where she introduced us to her buddies, Mario Andretti and Paul Newman, prior to the race. But that day she was rooting with us . . . for Scott.

Just putting an Indy car on the track for a season was feat itself. Racing was prohibitively expensive. Just getting a car on the track was exorbitant, let alone making it competitive. Without a corporate sponsor to fund their costly programs, racing teams don't stand a chance. With companies such as Beatrice Foods providing millions of dollars in support for front-tier drivers like Andretti, it made it tough for the second-tier drivers like Brayton at the time to catch up. So when young Scott of Coldwater, Michigan, set out to bring in a sponsor, he needed a jump start from us.

He hired us to run a publicity campaign whose ultimate goal was obtaining a sponsor for the Indy 500 that year. We kicked off our campaign with the *World's Fastest Billboard*, bringing Brayton and his Indy car into New York City to unveil it before a luncheon at Tavern on the Green. Painted on the side of his car was our sign: *This Space for Rent . . . $750,000.* The next day, the country's largest newspaper—*The New York Daily News*—ran a story on Brayton with a picture of our pricey ad big as life.

The dean of auto racing writers, Chris Economake, wrote in *National Speed Sport News* about our publicity coup: *TransMedia got more racing ink than any other PR house in New York has ever secured for racing.* We also got the renown sports artist LeRoy Neiman to sketch Brayton that day, but the pièce de résistance was having Elke throw a cocktail party at her home in LA to wish Brayton success in the Long Beach Grand Prix. On race day, she tied a silk scarf around his neck for luck. The photographers ate it up. Our race for a sponsor was on its final lap. Everything imaginable crossed our minds. Brayton's engine was a Buick, so we played up "American made" at a time when imports were clobbering Detroit.

We pitched his color, orange, to the Florida Citrus Commission: "The Fastest Thirst Quencher." To a New Jersey bank, we proposed having Brayton zip through their drive-ins in his Indy car. It didn't end there. Racing . . . Speed. The ideas whizzed by until just before the start of the Indy 500 that year, the prized ad space on the side of his Indy car went to . . . Hardee's.

Scott was a playful sort of guy. Always clowning. A regular joker! Most of the time, it was an endearing quality of his. But sometimes it was terrifying. Once, he and I were driving along Pacific Coast Highway when, for the fun of it, he floored the accelerator. Hurtling north at 90 m.p.h., I was on the passenger side looking over the precipitous cliff. The whiter I got from fear, the harder he'd laugh. *C'mon, cut it out. I mean it. Slow down, damn it,* I yelled. He slowed down finally, collapsing in laughter. I started to breathe again.

To Scott, it was harmless fun. Driving 90 m.p.h. was crawling. And on May 17, 1996, he was driving a lot faster. He was the Indy 500 pole-sitter and would have been the most experienced driver in the upcoming race. He was on a practice run, going 230 m.p.h. into Turn 2, when the right rear tire blew on his 1995 Lola-Menard. It sent him crashing backward into the wall. He died 33 minutes later. He became the 40th Indy 500 driver to die during practice, qualifications or in the race. I hope there's a track up in heaven for him.

Around the same time I was spinning a romance between Scott and Elke, I created and produced a shop-at-home videotape distributed at video rental stores called *Shop Around The World With Elke*. On our way back from Germany after shooting the pilot at her home outside Erlangen, plus some scenes at the nearby Rosenthal China showroom in Nuremberg, we accompanied her down to the Las Hadas Resort, where the film *10* starring Bo Derek, was made, near Manzanillo, Mexico.

I had arranged for *Playboy* Magazine to do a photo shoot of her, a sort of sequel to one *Playboy* had done years before when she was at the height of her career as a sexy co-star in films like *The Prize* with Paul Newman. As far as we were concerned Elke was still stunningly attractive. And beguiling. She'd rattle away describing to me how the shoot was going and about the silhouette shots at dusk, but I wouldn't hear a word she was saying. I was doing all I could just to maintain eye contact with her as she paced the floor of her Las Hadas suite rubbing oil on her huge bouncing naked breasts.

When she wasn't making us nervous, she'd make us laugh. She'd go behind the curtain of her boudoir, open it and present herself flamboyantly wearing nothing but her bikini bottom with a hair piece sticking out from the crotch. We'd all howl with laughter. Now in her 50s, she was still in fine shape. The curves were all still there in the right places. So was the firmness of her arms and legs from playing so much tennis. Her broad shoulders were sturdy as the Berlin Wall. And that erect posture made her statuesque. We'd go out on deep-sea fishing trips and she'd stand motionless at the very tip of the bow, leaning into the wind, looking straight ahead as if she were the vessel's ornament, a Neptunian Nymph rising and falling in a choppy sea. Watching her made us all seasick.

Wait. We're back at the reception area. How did Famous Amos get into our virtual tableau? I worked with Wally years ago promoting literacy before he got into financial difficulties and had to sell off his *Famous* name and cookie business. Wally would've chuckled at what I asked the valet tonight at the Ritz Carlton. *There's going to be a thousand people here tomorrow night*, he said expansively. *Barbara Bush is coming to speak on literacy. Oh*, I said. I*s she for or against it?* (rim shot) A couple of years ago, I got Wally to address a conference of adult and community education teachers in Florida sponsored by our client, Alamo Rent A Car. They were never more inspired. Wally's a lot better at inspiring than managing, however, which is how he lost his cookies. But now Wally's battling back. This indefatigable ex-William Morris agent already has had eight lives. Now he's starting all over with *Uncle Noname Gourmet Non-Fat Muffins.* He's no pup anymore, but he can still bark at you if you walk past his bakery products in the supermarket. If you want to learn promotion, watch Wally. Right now, he's watching Melinda Bonk smear herself with wild yam cream. She's the current client who wrote a book about *Controlling Hormones Naturally: My Journey for Solutions to PMS, Menopause & Osteoporosis With Wild Yam.* I don't have to tell you how *excited* women are about the wonders of wild yam.

21

**The man's a by-God spellbinder.
I haven't seen Iowa people get so excited since the
night Frank Dobson and Strangler Lewis lay on a mat
for three and a half hours without moving a muscle. . .
I want that man's credentials!
–The Music Man**

lso creaming himself, like Julio Iglesias caresses himself when
he sings *Crazy*, is Hydron Harvey. Harvey Tauman is QVC's
smooth-faced, smooth-talking ebullient king of skin care. He's
so moisturized, if you shake hands, don't squeeze too hard or it'll pop
out. In the past three years, Harvey has popped over $50 million worth
of tubes into the dry, chapped hands of QVC viewers. He pitches his
creams himself on-camera, exhorting viewers with the earnestness of
Sally Struthers' appeals to fight hunger and study auto repair. *Please,
just try it,* Harvey implores an elderly shut-in from Des Moines. *It'll
work miracles for you, dear. And make your skin moist, younger looking
and wrinkle free. It's a facelift in a bottle.* Just listen to this spell-bind-
ing Music Man of Skin Care and he'll convince you his miracle creams
will do everything but tie your shoe laces in the morning. That's right.

His creams will reach down through your pores and stop arthritic pain in your fingers so you can lace up and face up to the world.

Harvey can switch from salesman to scientist and back again. He explains that Hydron works so well because it contains a patented, secret polymer that keeps wonderful ingredients floating on your skin, allowing air in, so your skin'll breathe, but the healing, moisturizing, pain-relieving stuff won't perspire away because the polymer is water insoluble. No question about it. Harvey deserves an IgNobel Prize from Harvard University. Last year Ellen Kleinst from Nuuk, Greenland, and Harold Moi of Oslo, Norway, won it for their paper published in Genitourinary Medicine on "Transmission of Gonorrhea through an Inflatable Doll." If Harvey wanted to, he could sell Inflatable Dolls on QVC with or without gonorrhea. He's that persuasive. Amid a market glut of soap shops scenting up America's malls, undaunted Harvey keeps scoring hit after direct hit with that huge amorphous mass of compulsive, cubic-zirconized shop-at-home TV faithful glued to QVC.

The Nation's largest video retailer thought so much of Harvey (and the numbers he generates) that it bought 500,000 shares of stock in his NASDAQ-listed company, Hydron Technologies, Inc. Meanwhile, everywhere else, the personal care business is outpacing demand by so much that it is endangering the survival of such mall retailers as Nature's Elements, Garden Botanika and H2O Plus. But not Harvey. He thrives on TV and lives in the warm after glow of self appreciation and terminal narcissism.

And he appears younger, more radiant and water insoluble every time you see him. Some attribute Harvey's youthful appearance to the many Hydron creams with which he coats himself; others attribute his new-found youthfulness to a shapely mentorita about half his age, who moved in with him after his wife died suddenly about a year ago. And like father, like son, Richard Tauman, Hydron Technologies' CFO, also is in age remission, shedding pounds and looking more boyish by the minute since he met and started dating the account executive we assigned to the Hydron account, a prissy Aphrodite named Pam. She came to us from Colorado. Told us she had done publicity for

The Pike's Peak Auto Hill Climb, but later confessed what that meant. She was crowned "Miss Pike's Peak" once. We were familiar with the event. We once hired Elke Sommer to represent one of our erstwhile clients, a California company that made a carburetor for the aftermarket called "The Predator." The Predator was co-sponsor of the hill climb with Jolly Ranchers Candies, recently acquired by Hershey's.

And now Miss Pike's Peak, a 24-year-old Army brat whom we were paying $26,000 a year and whose father thanked me profusely for giving her a job, came in to work one day flashing a 4 carat diamond ring that Richard had given her. I figured we'd have the Hydron account for life, but that naive thought shortly got creamed. I received a letter from Richard informing us that henceforth they were taking all public relations functions in-house. Pam resigned and moved in with Richard.

Someone I'd like you to meet now is Doctor Mitchell Gaynor from Strang-Cornell Medical Center. He's the author of *Healing Essence: A Cancer Doctor's Practical Program for Hope and Recovery.* He heals cancer patients beyond hope with the essence of self-love. Be very still if you see him playing his Tibetan Singing Bowls. He says they produce the purest sounds yet developed for eliminating stress. Next to him are a pair of my favorite doctors, Klatz and Goldman. They're country's leading anti-aging activists. Dr. Ronald Klatz is President of the American Academy of Anti-Aging Medicine. The one with the muscles is Dr. Robert Goldman, President of the National Academy of Sports Medicine. He holds a world record for doing the most handstand pushups. Try one! We're promoting their book *Stopping The Clock* in which they tell why many of us will live past 100. And we can enjoy every minute if we learn how to halt or reverse the damage caused by aging, which is possible starting today with the amazing benefits of estrogen replacement, miraculous melatonin and DHEA, plus vitamins and minerals. They've made a believer out of me. I took their longevity test. According to my score, I'm going to live to 92. I swear they're geniuses. But I already know how I'm going to die. I'm going to be run over by a 150-year-old headless motorist from Century Village, Florida. You wait and see!

Now, don't be frightened. That skinny guy fiddling with the revolver is the inventor of SAF-T-LOCK. He's a spittin' image of Barnaby Jones. He is checking the patented combination lock mounted on his firearm. When it's locked, it can't be removed without destroying the gun. And if he needs to use it in a hurry, he can unlock it seconds. And in our burglar-phobic society it can save lives. As homes across America become arsenals, it can prevent children from shooting themselves or their playmates. And if President Clinton has his way and manages to get legislation through Congress requiring gun locks on all firearms to protect kids, Frank Brooks is going to be a rich man. Meanwhile, we came up with a campaign that was generating national press. We started to put out the spin that responsible gun ownership involves putting locks on firearms. Just as you wouldn't leave your front door unlocked, why wouldn't you also lock up something as potentially deadly as your gun? What's all this got to do with alternative health? How long do you think you and your loved ones are going stay healthy with a loaded gun in the house without a lock on it? If you own a firearm, for God's sake, keep a lock on it so your kids can be safe. After his stock hit $20 a share, to save a few thousand bucks a month, Barnaby terminates our services. I guess he figured he didn't need us anymore. Yet the share price drops to $3 and so far he has spent nearly $4 million to generate $50,000 in sales. We feel bad for Barnaby. He's got a great product. He knows a lot about locks, but crap about marketing. I wish he had listened to us. But no, he had to go and shoot himself in the foot . . . with a locked firearm.

The fit-looking chap in the yoga position with his eyes closed is Chris Kilham. He just returned from China where people use herbs the way we use aspirin. There are herbal remedies for just about everything. Kilham wants mainstream America to eat more plant-derived material, such as leaves, barks, berries, roots and stems. Plants contain compounds thought for centuries to be beneficial to health, from garlic to peppermint. Today herbs are being discovered by consumers, initially in health food stores and now coming to your neighborhood supermarket.

Ironically the benefits are being discovered in the rain forests by researchers for drug companies. Most pharmaceutical products originally have come from plants, but have been synthetically modified so they can be patented and sold as drugs at exorbitant prices. So in a weird way, out of their own self interest, drug companies might be helping to save our environment. Kilham has written many books, among them *The Whole Food Bible* and *In Search of The New Age*, a spoof of new age alternative cultures, and books on yoga, including *The Five Tibetans*, about a system of yoga exercises from Tibet. When he wants to relax, Kilham mixes himself an herbal cocktail of ginger, ginseng, bee pollen, royal jelly, ginkgo, extracts of medicinal mushrooms, and mixes it up in fresh juice or water. No one can say Kilham lacks energy. In his mid 40s he's an expert in martial arts, practices and teaches yoga, kayaking and body surfing. He snorkels, goes on hiking expeditions in the Himalayan foothills and up in the Sierras. Right now he's either meditating or taking a nap.

Some of you skeptics probably think that a few of our clients are merely modern-day medicine men hawking elixirs, magic potions, magic dust and tonics from their wagons. Others of you will kneel reverently before their wild yams, grapeseed extracts, shark cartilage, melatonin, antioxidant vitamin supplements or hormone replacement therapy. You see a brave new world, a promised land of enlightened 21st century all-natural medicine. Wherever you are along the spectrum of belief, know that I personally make no judgments or claims. This is merely a serendipitous journey of a spin man from *snap, crackle* and *pop* to Tibetan Singing Bowls.

22

Puff The Magic Dragon

Now in mid life, I've ventured boldly out to where no mainstream PR man has gone. I'm sailing unchartered waters, promoting alternative medicine, intriguing flotsam along its tributaries I hardly understand, some leading to the occult, to weird therapies and cure-alls, but ever outward to the entrepreneurial frontier. Maybe too far outward! Am I Danny Rose in a coonskin cap? Our firm represents some of the men and women on the frontier of science—some might say the *fringe*. But I prefer to think of them as soldiers on the front lines fighting PMS, incontinence, male impotence and cancer. Never mind the cigarette packs bulging in their shirt pockets or the small bottle of capsules they'll pull out of a desk drawer to cure *this* or another bottle from another drawer to cure *that*. Try to understand. Indulge a publicist who would like to believe in his client's miracles, who would like to think he is representing people who are sound of mind and pure of heart. Excuse his occasional hyperbole and transparent schemes and artifice he might use to perk up an idea with the finesse of a Caterpillar tractor. Like hiring Morton Downy Jr. as a spokesperson for LungCheck.

Downy was a natural for the role. He had been a four-pack-a-day smoker. He estimated he had taken well over a billion puffs on cigarettes. *It was like I was under a car sucking on the exhaust pipe for years.* Early in 1996, surgeons had removed almost three-quarters of his cancerous right lung. He flipped when we tracked him down and told him about LungCheck. It was state-of-the-art sputum cytology with a portable spittoon that you spat in and sent away for a speedy analysis. By analyzing cells coughed up from the lining of your lungs, doctors could predict the onset of lung cancer. *This is the beginning of the defeat of smoking and lung cancer*, he declared on CNBC's *America After Hours*. It was one of more than 50 broadcast hits we had gotten for the product nationwide and around the world on Brazilian and German television. We got a big story in *The New York Daily News* and Downey got so worked up, he spilled sputum on himself on *FOX After Breakfast*. We had the media jumping all over LungCheck.

We had staged a perfect news conference at The Strang Cancer Prevention Center at Cornell in Manhattan. Expecting a big press turnout, they had wanted to move it to a larger room, but I persuaded them to stay where they were so it would look more packed with TV crews, reporters and photographers. We even had Strang's Dr. Mitchel Gaynor booked on *Good Morning America* so he could praise LungCheck as an effective test for early detection of lung cancer.

We did until it fell apart when Strang's chief researcher was overly cautious and guarded in her remarks in a pre-interview. Scientists and lawyers! They're the bane of PR people. If they're not complicating and qualifying, they're downplaying until it's not a story anymore. Maybe LungCheck is a solution. Maybe not. But at least let's get the news out that it exists.

Fortunately for maybe thousands of smokers who might be helped by it, we got LungCheck a ton of press. It just might help someone avoid the horrors of lung cancer. And if we save just one lung out of all of this hoopla, I'm thrilled. And you can bet we'll go on promoting the hell out of it. These days we're promoting lots of medical doctors as a belt tightens around health care in this country, diminishing their revenues and forcing them to market themselves like lawyers.

We got Dr. Doug Stringham, an orthopedic surgeon client, on *Discovery* performing his carticel transplant knee surgery. And adorable Dr. Hernandez, the plastic surgeon, into major glamour magazines. And Dr. Richard Grable, the inventor of Imaging Diagnostic Systems's laser mammography, on ABC. And Rexall's Armend Szmulewitz on CBS with a heart transplant patient who says she's able to do things today she was never able to do because of the Vitamin C product she takes, supplied by independent distributors of Rexall Showcase International.

23

Searching For That Fountain Of Youth

As a mainstream PR man, promoting medical specialists seemed proper enough. It was not my intention to journey this far out into the panacea zone . . . through the black hole of nutritional healing. I came to Florida as a publicist, not Ponce d'Leon. But what I discovered was rejuvenating. They say the country's 76 million Baby Boomers like their youth so much they're going to drag it with them into old age. Here I am in my late fifties, maybe in the springtime of my senility, dragging around this feeling I'm 20 years younger. Dr. Hernandez says her patients complain that they feel so much younger than they look, so they want face lifts. Is it because I'm one of the youngest persons around my condo swimming pool? If one of my retired neighbors ever asked me to *run to the store,* would I hop out of my beach chair? Have I discovered a fountain of remedies to slow down the aging process? As an ex-journalist, I'm not altogether gullible about this. But I'm drinking optimistically from that fountain. And I suggest you do, too. Or look at the alternative. And don't be dismayed by the paradox of people with bags under their eyes, protruding bellies and receding hairlines promoting a panoply of anti-aging products. Talk about rainbows, they're the mother of all coalitions. The chain smokers, couch potatoes and alcoholics running companies that sell alternative health products . . . they're the champions, the exploiters and the profiteers of *entreprenutritionalism.* And many of them, God help us, are our clients. We promote their so-called cures and medical breakthroughs on news wires and in the hundreds of queries and news releases we send each week to writers and producers across the country each week. We book their for-hire "health experts" on countless radio and television programs nationwide and, until they're proven guilty or looney, we're their advocates. Yet, I'm realistic enough to know what a placebo is. Is the herbal drink's effectiveness due to the herbs? Or our faith in them?

A group of school teachers once were told certain of their students had high IQs, though in reality their intelligence was just average. None the less, the teachers tended to give higher grades to those students whom they thought had high IQs. So, do we tend to get what we expect? Is alternative medicine such a self fulfilling prophesy? Maybe. But I also believe that in the court of public opinion, it's entitled to a vigorous defense. Yet when a reporter asks what vitamins do for people, I'm not so dogmatic that I can't smile when a doctor answers: *It gives them expensive urine.*

· · ·

Today the race is on to find the antidote to aging. Already uncovered in such humble organisms as yeast, worms and fruit flies are a dozen longevity genes that can dramatically increase their life span. Can corresponding genes in human beings be manipulated to help us live longer, healthier lives? Who knows if that next bottle of capsules that comes out of somebody's musty desk drawer could be the magic elixir?

One of our clients is the American Academy of Anti Aging in Chicago. And as we promote them, we root for them. And we're not necessarily deterred if medical authorities haven't fully accepted all of our clients' theories yet. It wasn't from the authorities that we learned back in 1957 about the dangers of chemical additives and preservatives in our food. It was from one of Alternative Medicine's bibles—*Prevention* magazine. *Prevention* warned us long before it was a national issue. And in 1969, *Prevention* alerted us to the health hazards of DDT—a full 10 years before the government ban. And it linked heart disease and cancer to unhealthful foods in the American diet long before doctors saw the connection. *Prevention* readers also were among the first to discover the cholesterol-lowering effects of fiber foods like oat bran.

So it's been the commoners of alternative medicine, not the medical aristocracy, that's been promoting vitamin supplements for decades, plus low-fat eating, exercise, cancer prevention, stress control, Omega 3s or nutritional healing. And pointing out unnecessary medical procedures and the risks of women taking synthetic forms of naturally occurring hormones. So you tell me whom we should and should not promote?

24

Spinning Down The Amazon

In the late '80s, we felt like adventurers who had rushed to a far-off frontier. Only we had gone in the opposite direction from the tributaries of Bonanza Creek. Instead of the frozen north, we were down on a much warmer Klondike panning for clients. One of our earliest strikes in South Florida was a pot-bellied Peruvian Indian. Ney Piniero had to be one of the most colorful clients ever washed out of the Florida gravel. But this happy-go-lucky entrepreneur was no bonanza. He was a short, chunky Indian beset by health problems and living in virtual penury when we found him, or rather when he speared us out of the *Yellow Pages* like one of his catfish or piranha from the Amazon. His greatest wish was to immerse himself in a tank swarming with flesh-eating piranha. It would show his fearlessness and promote his exotic travel business, provided we could find a company willing to sponsor such a stunt. But I could just see the headline: PUBLICITY STUNT TURNS DEADLY; INDIAN EATEN ALIVE; PR MAN CHARGED WITH MANSLAUGHTER.

Ney had a unique travel business all right, but it had literally gone down the world's largest river. He was a daredevil explorer and guide who took wealthy thrill-seekers and adventurers on expeditions down the Amazon. There was only one problem. It was a one-way trip. His ramshackle raft never could make it back up the river. And his last

116

journey was so arduous and the accommodations so abominable that customers tried to sue him or have him arrested. But Ney assured us that he had resolved all the problems encountered on that trip and that his next expedition would go smoother and be well worth the $3,000 cost per person. He begged us to help him salvage his languishing Amazon excursions.

Although destitute, Ney was determined to take people back to the rich basin south of the Equator. His dream was to acquire a ship and convert it into a hospital that would sail along the river, providing medical treatment to natives from Peru to the Atlantic through Venezuela, Ecuador, Colombia, Bolivia and Brazil and along the twisting tributaries of Japura, Jurua, Madeira, Negro, Purus, Tocantins and Xingu. His round, jowly face and pot belly, together with his short stature, reminded me of Lou Costello, the comedian, up the creek without a paddle. I think that's partly why we became so fond of him. As a kid, I adored Abbott & Costello films and their Who's-On-First routines and slapstick. But one look at Ney and you knew he'd never make it to first on his own. He'd been waiting all his life for flies to be hit to him in his outfield of dreams, but he never caught one. In our hearts we knew we were never going to strike it rich with Ney, but we wanted to help this scruffy little Peruvian Indian somehow. He was fun and the trip he was offering was definitely something unusual enough to promote at a fund-raiser in Palm Beach where the socialites were always looking for something different to auction off for charity. So for the hell of it, we decided to help Ney get back on his bare feet and out on the Amazon again. As payment for our services, we accepted a commission on trips that he sold as a result of our efforts.

His river craft was a home-made floating raft with a few cabins and even fewer amenities. It was built upstream for a one-way voyage. Ney served as captain, travel agent, cook, head waiter, entertainer and guide for those few brave souls who could afford this once-in-a-lifetime excursion into the lush and fertile Amazon basin teaming with vegetation, hardwood trees, rare plants, insects, birds, fish, reptiles, tapirs, tropical otters, hundred-pound rodents, anteaters and numerous kinds of monkeys. It would float from Peru to journey's end in Brazil, where the excursion survivors, if there were any, then hopped on a plane for the flight back to civilization.

When I offered one of Ney's trips for two down the Amazon to be auctioned off, socialite Rutilia Poli Burck was absolutely titillated. Rutilia, an Italian countess, was a direct descendent of another far-out explorer, Marco Polo. She chaired the auction committee for a Red Cross benefit and asked if I would personally auction it off, which I agreed to do on the condition that Ney could also be present dressed in his native garb, have dinner and show his artifacts from the Amazon? *Why of course. Bring him with you,* Rutilia said. *He'll be fun.* So with one of Ney's Amazonian paddles in my hand, I walked up to the podium in my black tie and proceeded to excite the audience with this once-in-a-lifetime opportunity for adventure on the Amazon. When I finished describing it, people started bidding so fiercely you'd think they were Vietnamese refugees and Ney's Kon-Tiki was the last boat out of Saigon. *Five hundred dollars from the athletic-looking young gentleman to my left. Do I hear one thousand? Thank you, Madam. The bid is one thousand. Do I hear fifteen hundred?* And on it went until I realized that one of the bidders was a pale gentlemen in his eighties who seemed hell bent to buy this trip for himself and his elderly wife. Was he crazy? How long could these two old birds last south of the Equator in the blazing heat and humidity of the mosquito-infested Amazon? And suddenly he's the top bidder at $7,500. Now I'm praying the younger man will top it. I'm helping the Red Cross all right: raising funds, providing victims. There's got to be someone more apt to survive this trip who'll outbid him. My God, this is no joke, I thought. This trip will certainly kill these two old people and I'll be responsible for selling it to them. If it weren't for me, they'd still be alive. I could see headlines screaming: PR MAN SENDS SWEET ELDERLY COUPLE TO HORRIBLE DEATH IN THE AMAZON. *I have seventy five hundred. Do I hear eight thousand? Please, do I hear seventy-nine hundred for the Red Cross? Anybody? You sir?* to the fit young man. I'm really sweating now. *Okay, seventy-six hundred for a trip of a lifetime? Seventy five five? No? Seventy-five going once.* Please don't do this to me! *Seventy five going twice.* No, this can't be happening! *Sold to the gentleman to my right.* To the frail, anemic-looking gentlemen and his wife, I said to myself, who won't last two hours in that heat and humidity on the Amazon. What have I done? I've auctioned them to die. I could already see the headline: PR MAN PUSHES SENIORS INTO PIRANHA INFESTED AMAZON.

To make matters worse, the old gentlemen who had bought the trip turns out to be a retired attorney. Now I've had it for sure. SUPREME COURT UPHOLDS $10 MILLION JUDGMENT AGAINST PR MAN! But fortunately he kept putting the trip off, which was a break because Ney was broke and couldn't afford to build another raft. Meanwhile, the Red Cross spent the $7,500 on helping victims of Hurricane Andrew. Rutilia Burck sold her villa and moved out of Palm Beach. We got busy with other clients and really didn't have a lot of time to help Ney anymore. Gradually we lost track of Ney. And the old man, who had been the successful high bidder, finally lost interest himself in going down the Amazon after his wife became ill. And then we heard that Ney wouldn't be taking anyone down the Amazon anymore. He had set up a non-profit foundation that was trying to acquire a moth-balled ship to convert into a hospital when he suffered a fatal heart attack. I think he was in his forties. If he had stayed on the Amazon, he probably would have lived to a hundred. But in Florida too many Cokes, burgers, fries and pancakes had done him in. Civilization speared him through the heart.

Mind Over Behind

To our bulging Florida client roster, we add one of the state's oldest and largest law firms, Gunster Yoakley Valdes-Fauli & Stewart, after it won a landmark case against 19 international co-conspirators illegally importing and marketing prescription drugs in the U.S. They want more pharmaceutical clients, so we get them featured in *Drug Store News*, *Chain Drug Review* and *Pharmaceutical Executive Magazine*. The University of Miami/Jackson Memorial Medical Center retains us to help them to raise funds for a needed Pediatric Bone Marrow Transplant Center, for which we get Rexall Sundown to provide $300,000. And Dr. Edward E. Eckert retains us to promote his Kosher-organic restaurant, *Whole Earth Market*, and his upcoming book, *The Making of a Gynecologist: Mind*

Over Behind. Dr. Eckert has his eye on one of our account executives, but she tells him *you'll never get me in your stirrups.* We had quite a time convincing a board of rabbis that his kosher market was kosher. The *Jewish Times* reported that the sign on the window of the market had boasted kosher food prematurely and the chair of the Palm Beach County Va'ad Hakashrut said the health food store has yet to be certified. It was all a mistake that we quickly straightened out.

The sign was supposed to have said the restaurant was in the process of becoming kosher, but Mashgiach Yehuda Greenberg, who supervised the Kosher Resorts that provide Disney World with its kosher foods, technically hadn't donned his goggles and blow-torched the pots and pans yet. The process is necessary to achieve Kashrut, the highest level of Kosher necessary to accommodate the strictest orthodox jews. The flap lasted only a week in the Jewish press. After the blow-torching was done, all cooking utensils were dipped into the heated vat of water called the Hagallah, and then into cold water, and the entire kitchen was gated so no one could enter during shabbos. So you can believe it. This place is as kosher as you can get. And you have this Irishman's word that you'll never find a restaurant as immaculate. Because we're a firm that thrives on synergy, we organized a health symposium at Dr. Eckert's market and plugged in as one of the presenters our anti-aging client, Dr. Ron Klatz. Several local TV stations were on their way to cover it until a double murder swept them away. One of our account executives called assignment desks to find out if it involved children with firearms. The *Rolanda* Show was looking for such an angle for Saf T Lok, our child-proof lock for firearms.

Though located way down on the Florida peninsula, our reputation is spreading across the country. We have clients now from Arizona to New York. Even the Strang Cancer Prevention Center at Cornell Medical Center up in New York, hearing about our effectiveness in generating national publicity, retained us to do it for them. Of course, like most firms, we have had our sprinkling of oddballs like Dr. Shapiro's Hair Transplant Institutes. In a pinch, I substituted for one of Dr. Shapiro's pincushions. Thousands of TV viewers saw my bald spot disappear on WPTV in West Palm Beach one micro graft at a time. It proves publicists will do anything for a placement, especially vain ones. We represented Bill Knight, a hard-driving land developer, who wanted us to convince residents that a humongous shopping center would make an ideal neighbor. We couldn't do it. And I almost got a brick on my head. And we went to bat for Leonard Briscoe, a tall, affable black builder whom I felt was being vilified for ushering in a sea change in the way public housing was built and maintained in America. Briscoe had created beautiful gated communities with grassy knolls and swimming pools and amenities usually accorded middle class apartment dwellers, not the working poor. But in the process, he had gotten too chummy with HUD officials. Charges that he had made bribes in return for privileged contracts and concessions were swirling and drowning out the good he had done in terms of vastly improved HUD housing. Our strategy was to crystallize the good side of Briscoe and focus on his many achievements. We created a video that depicted them. It included testimonials by satisfied tenants who praised Briscoe for the uplifting surroundings in which they were living.

And up in his Trump Tower apartment I prepped him for appearances before a Congressional committee investigating HUD. At the same time, we staged rallies in West Palm Beach in his support and got leaders in the Black community to brand allegations against him as racially motivated. For a while the press coverage turned positive and it looked as if Briscoe might survive. But the charges turned to indictments and eventually our tall, congenial client went to jail. Alas, there are limits what a spin man can do. You can shade reality. Put a positive spin on it. You can even fight the facts for a while, but ultimately you can't change them. The truth will out do you every time. Still I still feel bad for Briscoe. He's the kind of man who has the talent and courage the black community needs. Yet he did some things perhaps he shouldn't have. And he got caught. Will it make him a wiser builder? Will he get a second chance? I hope so. Beyond these few setbacks, our PR business is booming. Even F. Lee Bailey, who we often see wandering around the Ritz Carlton in Palm Beach, can't win 'em all. But why does he glower so? The other night he stood in the bar and just his pugnacious presence, we think, made a glass fall from a table, frightening a little German girl to tears. *He carries around those evil OJ spirts,* my wife says. Meanwhile our client list continues to expand and revenues double each year. And we're ensconced in our comfortable Boca Raton reviewing stand watching the parade of entrepreneurs, charlatans, strippers, huggers, healers, con artists, geniuses, Mafiosos, rock'n rollers, quacks, fakes and assorted nuts and even occasional evil spirts go passing by. Watching the parade with us is our spirited drum majorette, Margie Adelman.

25

Tales Of "The Urine Lady"

Margie is a short, busty, high-powered publicist who bulls her way onto broadcast programs like a fullback punching through the line of scrimmage. When other publicists are blocked, she finds the hole and sails through it like a Tony Dorsett. And she has gained more media yardage for our clients than anyone else on our publicity team. She also comes up with great copy lines like *We make love better* for a chain of impotency treatment centers. And this triple entente title for a radio show we created for them—*Sex Matters*. Because she's such a consistent high scorer, we made her president of our firm and I kicked myself upstairs to chairman. In another life, however, she kow-towed to gurus and was an alternative health missionary known as "The Urine Lady."

She gave lectures to AIDS patients on urine therapy and traveled worldwide researching its benefits, including a stint in India where she met one of the world's most famous pee drinkers, the 98-year-old ex-prime minister Moraji DeSai. So, around the same time we were launching our PR firm in New York, Margie was starting the urine therapy movement in the early 1980s. A good pot of pee, or autoimmune buccal therapy, is based on the theory that the biochemicals that we expel through our bladder are in the exact proportion needed by our body to fight disease. So why not put them back? Because it's exactly what your body needs to heal itself, as the theory goes, it's healthful to drink your own urine. Needless to say, it's a controversial theory. Margie blushes a little when she talks about it today, but back then she'd respond to an incredulous press citing the analogy of dead leaves remineralizing the soil. *The most luscious forests in the world are not landscaped. Why would you flush away something your body expels that's so beneficial?* she would ask.

And in the same town where I had once acted on stage, in Coconut Grove, Margie was the publicist for Burton Goldberg, the Grove's real estate mogul who spent millions of his own fortune to publish *The Definitive Guide to Alternative Medicine*. A chapter of Margie's alternative lifestyle she prefers to forget is when she was the publicist for Basil Wainright, the father of rectal insufflation or *King Con*, as the *Sun-Sentinel* dubbed him some years ago.

Wainright, who currently is a fugitive from the law, was operating an unlicensed rectal insufflation practice out of a private home in a residential community in Fort Lauderdale. Patients would come in Mercedes and Jaguars, in wheelchairs and on crutches all hours of the night to this house he rented where he stuck a catheter up their rectums and pumped them full of ozone in a kind of superoxygenated enema that would elate patients whose faces would actually glow when they left. *It was like they were coming to a church and he was their Messiah who could heal the sick through their rectums.* It lasted until a SWAT team raided the place and arrested Wainright for practicing medicine without a license.

Wainright's theory was that the ozone, or O^3, which is oxygen with a singlet oxygen molecule kicker, would penetrate the colon wall and be absored in the blood, losing its free radical kicker that would then go off scavanging for weaker, less stable free radical cells. When it found them, it would attach itself and annihilate them, thus killing viruses and regenerating nerves. In media appearances Margie arranged, such as on *Dr. Gary Null's Show* heard by 14 million people in 125 markets, as well as on television shows and in interviews with newspapers, Wainright touted his controversial theory until he was put behind bars.

Margie has no connection any more with the infamous Basil Wainright, but oxygen is a hard thing to let go of. The first week she joined our firm she talked us into having her friend John Taggert install ultra violet oxygen producing light bulbs that are bacteriostatic. So to this day we have the most oxygen-rich, pollutant-free public relations firm in the country.

26

Come Aboard, We've Got Some Hot Cocoa For You

People often ask where we get our public relations clients from. The answer is from several places. Some come in as referrals from satisfied clients. Some find us in the *Yellow Pages*. And a few I pluck from rough waters. My wife calls it ambulance chasing, but to me, it's the PR Coast Guard to the rescue. And as every hurricane-rattled Floridian knows, disaster is a seller's market. So each morning I patrol the business pages of the morning newspapers searching for wreckage, listening for an SOS. Dead ahead, a company torpedoed by a negative story. Sometimes it's unfair as hell. A security analyst downgrades its stock. The market overreacts. The share price dives. Or quarterly earnings are a penny below estimates. Or sales are just a little off. Or some other *disaster* befalls a corporate ship, knocking it off course, forcing its CEO and crew to put on their life jackets and take their battle stations. I'll come along and spot them bobbing in chilly oil-slick waters. *Come on board, we've got some hot cocoa for you people.* I'll call them and introduce myself as a public relations pro. An expert in crisis management. I know exactly what they're going through. I know the reporter who wrote the story. I can help them save their ship. I've been through this many times with other clients and it has turned out well. I'll throw them a life saver. Pull them onboard. And serve them our nice hot cocoa. It was Saturday. I was cruising the columns in *The Palm Beach Post* when I saw this alarming report about Margarita y Amigas. Over 600 people had gotten sick from salmonella poisoning at the Palm Beach Gardens eatery. If any business needed a life raft fast, they did. So I rushed to the phone and called the restaurant. To my surprise, the owner, Bob McFadden, answered. He sounded like a man who could use a cup of hot cocoa. I said I'd like to come over and talk with him. Wearily, he said okay. I got dressed, stuck a contract in my pocket and headed out in my Jaguar XJS convertible, amphibious rescue cutter. When I arrived at Margarita y Amigas, I found McFadden to be in a jovial mood, which was surprising since his restaurant had just set a record for causing the most cases of salmonella poisoning ever at a Florida eatery. "Would you like a killer chicken sandwich?" he asked me. It was clearly an attempt at gallows humor. "No thanks," I told him. Actually, I was afraid to touch anything.

I was there to give him some PR advice on how to manage a crisis, not to add to his record. We sat down and talked. He told me he always wanted to run a world-famous restaurant, but he didn't have quite this in mind. Stories about Margarita y Amigas had even hit the papers in Bosnia. I whipped out a contract—we call it an *Agreement*—and he agreed to pay a monthly fee if we could get the press off his back so he could concentrate on salvaging his business.

Rescuing Margarita Salmonita Ole!

A single day had nearly demolished all that McFadden had spent more than a decade building. He had run Margarita y Amigas, a popular Palm Beach Gardens, Florida, Mexican restaurant without incident for 14 years until last August. After a busy evening where he served 1,100 dinners, the restaurateur began to receive calls from customers complaining of feeling ill. That was just the tip of an iceberg that had ripped a giant gash in the side of his business. Now he was floundering. More than 180 cases of salmonella poisoning had been reported, and the media had broadcast McFadden's misfortune worldwide. It was a public relations nightmare that could have permanently knocked him out.

The sheer number of people who became sick caught media attention, I was quoted in *Entrepreneur* magazine in March 1996, which published an anatomy of our PR rescue mission. McFadden retained us to manage the media crisis for him while he closed his restaurant for more than a week to thoroughly sanitize the kitchen and implement state-of-the art food handling measures. When he reopened, we helped him use the media attention to show patrons enjoying food and remaining healthy. That, plus a display of hundreds of letters of support from friends and patrons, turned the tide. Margarita's business is back up to about 80 percent of normal, and although he lost about $200,000, McFadden isn't panicked. *My landlord said not to worry about rent until we were back on our feet,* he said. *The grocery and meat companies said the same about their bills.*

McFadden told *Entrepreneur* that he would offer the same advice that his PR firm had given to him: *The best advice I can offer to entrepreneurs in a crisis is to be ethical, moral and a stand- up person who faces the problem and solves it.* Here are other tips that I give to business owners when a crisis strikes, which were reported in a sidebar story in *Entrepreneur*:

- Stay calm. It's natural to be agitated, but you don't want to project that image to the public. They need to perceive you as in command.

- Be responsive. Don't try to hide or withdraw from the limelight; that only makes the situation worse.

- Use the media to tell the public what's happening, what you are doing about it, and steps you are taking to prevent a reoccurrence.

- Focus on looking ahead rather than back and avoid getting defensive.

- Make sure the public knows about the people who support you through the crisis.

- Ensure that the crisis is interpreted as an isolated incident instead of a trend.

- Before a crisis hits, develop a crisis management plan. Choose a company spokesperson and identify vulnerable areas to determine what's most likely to go wrong.

And one more pointer, which I gave to the *Miami Herald,* in a story about the PR aftermath of TWA Flight 800's explosion shortly after takeoff from Kennedy International Airport:

- Whatever you do, respond quickly and be immediately assessable. Don't wait 24 hours like TWA did before providing substantive information to the press about a major disaster.

- And the bottom line is this. If there's nothing rotten in Denmark, then by all means invite reporters in to see Denmark.

27

They're Mugging Mother Teresa In My Salon

It was not the first time we represented a restaurant. Back in New York, we did some genteel publicity for one of the most charming restaurants on the upper East Side, Le Chantilly at 57th and Park Avenue. We got columnists Cindy and Joey Adams of the *New York Post* to do interviews there and celebrities like Rex Harrison to lunch there regularly. In keeping with the lovely murals of thoroughbred horse racing and other equestrian scenes around Chantilly, France, for which the restaurant was named, we invited top jockeys from Belmont and Aqueduct to dine there, and placed *who-was-seen-dining-at* items in the right columns read by the right people. Le Chantilly was one of a few clients we had on Manhattan's posh 57th Street in those days.

Another was Pierre Cardin's *Evolution Gallery* where we produced and promoted "A Tribute to Mother Teresa." The tribute was in the form of paintings by Indian artist M.F. Husain, who looked like a prophet who had strode right out of the Bible. He cut an ethereal figure in his white linen robe walking barefoot in the snow and slush around Manhattan in mid winter. He had thick white hair, a flowing white beard and a rugged face that looked like it had been chiseled from brownstone. He painted Mother Teresa's famous blue and white veil flowing in divine breezes. We got the artist featured on New York television and radio stations the week of his opening and handled every detail of his vernissage, from ordering the champagne to turning out the art press in New York. We persuaded the Cardin's gallery to host the party. And we got then U.N. Secretary General Javier Perez de Cuellar and other dignitaries to accept our invitations to the lavish reception. And we came within a brush stroke of creating an international scandal.

We had hired Baron Philippe de Moyer de Lasheraine to hang the show for us. About two hours before the reception was to start, Pierre Cardin walked in and was aghast. We had defiled his gallery. *Take them all down*, he ordered. *I won't have my gallery disgraced.* We looked at one another dumbfounded. He complained we had hung the pictures all wrong. Big pieces should be in the front, not hidden in the back. How stupid of us. The way Cardin carried on, it was as if we had pulled Mother Teresa into his salon and mugged her. It reminded me of a story about another mercurial maestro, Arturo Toscanini. One day during rehearsal, Toscanini got so upset over the way a violinist played a particular passage that he threw his baton into the air and stormed off the podium. He went to his dressing room, bolted the door and wouldn't come out. At the urging of fellow orchestra members, the offending violinist had to go up to the door and play the passage exactly as Toscanni had wanted it phrased. Then the door opened. The beaming maestro emerged. And returned to the podium triumphantly.

I asked this other maestro how he would have conducted the picture hanging. He glared at us, then spoke. *The large picture*, he snorted, pointing his artful index finger to an idyllic space over the entrance way, *IT GOES THERE!* Baron Philippe saw the same light as I did and he rushed to get the large painting. I went for the ladder. We hung it exactly where Cardin had pointed. *How's that?* I asked our petulant host. He was pacing, holding his chin in one hand, in deep perturbed thought. The red scarf draped over his shoulders flapped angrily at us. Waiting for the verdict, we cringed. Minutes were ticking away. The secretary general was probably putting on his bow tie already. I could imagine the United Nations demanding to know what PR firm was responsible for this profound insult to India and to Mother Teresa. Cardin turned and looked up at the large picture. *Yes!* We all breathed again. *And put that one over there!* We obeyed.

I could see Cardin beginning to rearrange all the pictures in his enveloping mind. *And this one goes here. That one there!* The finality. The decisiveness of his commands was awesome. He was in complete control of the battlefield. We were his warriors. And if he wished, we would hurl ourselves upon his sword. In less than two hours, we re-hung nearly 60 pictures. It was miraculous. Mother Teresa's veils were still flapping when we opened the doors. But it was an entirely new show. It was Cardin's show. Grandly, he greeted the press. Spoke eloquently about Husain's art, which he so admired—but had almost thrown out the door in a rage. And he waxed poetic about his deep affection for Mother Teresa, whose veils had flapped around that day as vigorously as Cardin's scarf. If anyone would like to see this mad-cappery, my son Andrew recorded it all on video tape. Pierre Cardin. He was our exalted ruler. What a guy!

The press that we got was so wonderful that other galleries hired us for their openings, including Edward Nahamkin Fine Arts and the Dyansen Gallery in Soho, where I met the people in black: the one-time prima ballerina Makarova, the prodigy pianist VanCliburn and the scarred and tortured Russian painter Chemiakin. And a steely German lady invited us to produce an art show in her $10 million apartment on the 64th floor of Trump Tower where she was building a swimming pool directly under The Donald's apartment. We called our event "Art In The Sky," benefitting living memorial scholarships for young people in Jewish studies programs. Each scholarship was given in the name of a child who died in the Holocaust. Rabbi Bernard Mandelbaum asked us to be the public relations firm for his Foundation for Future Generations. A non-Jew who was helping Jews, the Rabbi called me one of *The Righteous.* So I owe Cardin many thanks for those accounts.

Whenever I think of that swimming pool at Trump Tower, I can't help feeling sorry for poor Mrs. Katz who lived in the condo where we bought our first apartment in Florida. She only wanted a washer in her apartment. When the Condo Board refused to allow it, she went to court, but it cost her $5,000 out of her retirement savings when she lost. The judge said she and her handicapped husband had to resign themselves to using the communal laundry on the floor above. When you're rich, like the lady in Trump Tower, the world is your oyster. When you're not, you can choke on oysters.

Up to that art exhibition on the 64th floor we dragged poor old Huntington Hartford. After hours! I had never seen anyone snort as much coke as Hartford. He was a friend of Leonardo Parterson, who was a client of ours from Costa Rica. Despite his splashy lifestyle, we didn't think Leonardo was a drug dealer. His business was antiquity art. And business was good.

28

Whatever Happened To Leonardo?

Leonardo lived at the Olympic Towers opposite St. Patrick's Cathedral. He dealt with the world's biggest collectors like Hartford. He sometimes stayed down the street in a suite at The Helmsley's Palace, which we could never quite figure out. He was very religious and carried prayer beads. I met Leonardo in the sushi bar at the Century Plaza Hotel in Beverly Hills. After we struck up a friendly conversation, he asked me to guess what he did.

He was a black man with an entertaining personality. *You're a rock star?* He almost de-stooled himself laughing. He said he was an art dealer and asked if I would be his guest at the premiere of a film he was shooting. I said I'd be happy to and we parted. A couple of months later I received a first-class British Airways ticket in the mail—to Sydney, Australia. That's where his premiere was—on the other side of the world. To my wife's credit, she had enough faith in me to let me go off on this little adventure by myself. So I flew to Australia with stopovers in Honolulu and Tahiti. When I arrived, Leonardo had a driver pick me up and take me to the Seibold Terrace, where Liza Minelli and all the stars stayed. When I finally saw him the next morning, he hugged me as if I was a long-lost friend and he asked if I would introduce his film at the Sydney Opera House that evening. It was a film about Mayan Indians and art excavations in Mexico. I agreed. I was so jet-lagged, however, I have no recollection of what I spoke about that night, or what for me was that morning. He seemed pleased, nevertheless. He let me relax for a few days and I flew back to New York.

A few months later we arranged a party for 200 people at Regine's to show excerpts of the same film. We got Channel 5's Marian Etoile Watson to interview him about his digging for art in the jungles deep inside Mexico's Yucatan Peninsula. We did other special things for him and he paid us in art pieces. One was a cracked head held together by a rubber band around its forehead like a Pre-Columbian athlete wearing a sweat band. An appraiser said it was 2,000 years old.

Then one day Leonardo just took off. Plum disappeared! His wife asked us tentatively if he had owed us any money. No, he didn't owe us anything. *That's good*, she said relieved. He joined the nebulous ranks of persons who've passed through our lives like ships in the night or maybe trucks sideswiping each other. In that group are Prince Esterhazy, an alleged scion of the Austrian House of Esterhazy who carried a jewel-tipped walking stick and wanted us to help him to launch a cosmetics line. We put a marketing plan together for him, but dropped it in a hurry after receiving a letter from a law firm informing us that he was an imposter and we were risking a law suit. Another royal romantic was Prince Monyo, a Romanian sculptor who lived at Palm Beach's swanky Colony Hotel, owned three Rolls Royces and pursued women like a man with a hard-on dipped in bronze; Jim Fite, a mild-mannered inventor of an ordinary-looking park bench with the one bright exception that his *Glow Bench* could glow in the dark with advertising; Charles Svirk, who marketed a laser-guided golf putter with his partner George Lindemann Jr., a member of the U.S. equestrian team and a billionaire's son, who was convicted on charges related to the electrocution of show horses for insurance money; the whimsical and personable Mike Pinera of *In A Gadda Da Vida* and *Iron Butterfly* fame, the ethereal artist Husain and John Gotti's boyhood friend and employer. They all vanished from our lives just as suddenly as they had appeared. And maybe that was a good thing.

29

**In the morning, I'll be sober.
You, Madam, will still be ugly.
*—Winston Churchill***

Restaurants are difficult accounts. You have to contend with something akin to the overnight Nielsen ratings. They're called reservations. You're like a TV programmer living and dying with the overnights. As one executive with whom I worked at NBC put it, "I go to sleep every night with a knot in my stomach like I'm in the sixth grade and my report card's coming out the next day." Only with eateries you don't get a chance to sleep. You get a story published in the morning paper. And by that evening, if the owner doesn't see an increase in dinner reservations, you're in hot water. Restauranteurs typically have that kind of hard-headedness about publicity. You can forget the image stuff. Empty chairs are like carbon dioxide cylinders. They require continual filling. When waiters start to look forlornly at tables with empty chairs around them, you'd better start calling people to fill them. That's why we really don't relish restaurant accounts. Even when they're as splendid as *Churchill's*.

If you were watching the 1996 Honda Classic golf tournament on NBC, you might have seen it fly across your screen: our banner announcing that *Churchill's Pub & Restaurant* was opening soon. It got almost as much attention as the Goodyear Blimp at the Super Bowl. We had the airplane pulling our banner circle the tournament for over an hour. And NBC's viewers nationwide could see it on the wide shots of high arcing drives down the fairlane. It may even have been an historical stunt. The first ground-to-air-contact executed in a publicity campaign. We had Her Majesty Queen Elizabeth pointing up at the sign with her white-gloved finger as she walked among throngs of spectators.

Our queen was Judith Gindy, winner of the Queen Elizabeth look-alike contest sponsored by the *Miami Herald*, American Airlines and Intercontinental Hotels. Wearing her crown and ermine cape, she strode regally among her curious subjects in the gallery. A group of vacationing Scandinavian children even curtsied as scores of tourists asked for her autograph. It was a royal stunt, a throwback to the early days of PR when press agents did incredible things for attention, when PR was probably a lot more fun than it is today. *Churchill's* was the dream of Victoria Williamson, a tall, shapely, beautiful woman with dark-eyes, jet black hair, fair skin and a come hither smile that would make your shepherd's pie boil over. Bob Williamson, her husband, is a chain smoker who grins benignly at all around him. You'd grin too if you were the largest independent oil distributor in the U.S. When he talks, it's usually in a whispered, gravelly voice like he's sharing some top secret.

Once at a party at Ivana Trump's home in Palm Beach, Bob shared his succinct appraisal of her yacht. *It's a piece of shit.* When he saw only white wine being served, he nearly had a fit. *No scotch?* he asks one of the servers. *Only wine, sir.* Ivana was protecting her furnishings. I sent an SOS to his chauffeur on my portable phone. *You'd better hightail it over here with a Dewar's on the rocks.* When you're rich as Bob, your slightest desire can be a full-blown emergency for the minions around you. When Bob and Victoria married, Victoria was invited to be on *Oprah* in a segment on *Gold Diggers*, about women who marry older men for their money. And much to Bob's chagrin, the starry-eyed daughter of a Midwestern chiropractor accepts. She brings her hair dresser with her to Chicago and avows on national TV that in her case it was different. She didn't marry Bob for the cream-colored Bentley, the walnut-size diamonds, waterfront home, designer wardrobe or even the 126-foot yacht that Bob gave her to party on with her young friends. Hell no. It was for love. And 15 years later has proven her right as they are still married. Only now Bob is in his 70s and likes to retire early. And Victoria, still in her 30s, is sleepless in Fort Lauderdale. The corespondent in her life is *Churchill's.*

Every daylight minute and sleepless night, it intrudes into her inner-most thoughts. She stays up drinking champagne and telephoning people, starting in the East around Midnight and working her way West. Sheriff Nick Navarro, who was instrumental in bringing *COPS* to television and now runs a thriving private security business, thanks me to this day for having taken the pressure off him and his wife, Sharron. Victoria called them practically every night. Nick's a Cuban Italian. He told me: *We made her an offer she couldn't understand.*

Now Victoria awakens us, her publicists, after midnight to ask what's happening. I'd respond half asleep that there was a lot in the works. And she'd tell me about a another antique brass plate she just *stole* for a hundred dollars at one of the many flea markets she cruises daily, prowling for British antiques with which to decorate *Churchill's. And when it's polished, it's going to look magnificent over the bar, and couldn't I just picture it . . . and could we join her at a black-tie char-ity gala Saturday night . . . for a cruise Sunday on her yacht, and lunch tomorrow at the French Quarter . . . and please invite society columnist Betty Williams from the Sun-Sentinel?* And I'd say *yes, yes, yes, we'd love to, of course we'll come, certainly, thank you.* And pass out!

The Williamsons dock their sleek yacht (once featured in a James Bond film) in nearby *La Serena,* their luxurious waterfront home in Fort Lauderdale. If they're not cruising to Entebe with their friends Roy and Lea Black, Victoria is driving her Bentley to cocktail parties and fash-ion shows or she and Bob are being driven by Neil in their white Rolls Royce Limousine. Neil is their affable British butler and chauffeur. He and Andy, the first of many *Churchill's* managers, devote themselves to fulfilling Mrs. Williamson's continuous need for champagne. Neil was the inspiration behind *Churchill's.* It was his vision. But he was becoming a nervous wreck and developing a heart condition watching Mrs. Williamson implement it. It started with the odd location she selected, about 12 miles southwest of Fort Lauderdale in the cowboy community of Cooper City. But that's where Bob owned a shopping center and had reserved a corner space where Victoria could build her dream restaurant. It would be something to keep her occupied. An outlet for her boundless energy. But he didn't figure on quite such an expensive outlet. Victoria plowed millions of dollars of Bob's oil money into turning an empty space at an ordinary strip center next to a McDonald's into an opulent British Restaurant and Pub. But she went a little too far when she instituted a dress code that Cooper City's dungaree'd denizens resented. But Victoria stuck to her guns and to her husband's dismay, she cast out the shitkickers in their T-shirts and turned away anyone improperly attired. Bob wondered how many times would Roy and Lea and their friends drive all the way out to dine there?

The Blacks were among their closest friends. Black, who is frequently seen on *Geraldo* and *The Today Show* as a consultant to NBC, defended William Kennedy Smith in the first circus trial of a new era in which conservative daily newspapers slugged it out with supermarket tabloids and live courtroom testimony preempted afternoon soap operas on TV. And in those pre-O.J. days, many Americans got their first glimpse of prominence on trial and of the best defense money could buy. One of the jurors whom Black appealed to was Lea, Juror No. 1, a looker with long stringy blonde hair from Waco, Texas, who drove a Mercedes convertible around Palm Beach. Black met Lea for the first time socially at E. R. Bradley's Saloon in Palm Beach as the defense team celebrated Smith's bullet-train acquittal of rape charges. They were married two years later. If you stay up late, you can catch Lea in her glitzy infomercial for *Accent*, a pair of silicone-gel breast enhancers. They work much *better than duct tape.*

The Grand Opening was a smash. Bagpipes blared. Search lights beamed to the sky. Our emcee interviewed dignitaries, celebrities and movie stars who jammed the 5,100 square-foot eatery. Mr. Williamson looked *Bogey* in his white dinner jacket. Victoria was a shimmering contrast in black. Sir Freddie Laker was there. We raffled off a pair of tickets to his latest inaugural flight to London. (It had to return to Kennedy after developing engine trouble.)

Actor Steven Bauer finally made it after midnight. So did reporters for the *Miami Herald* and *Sun-Sentinel*. But where were the TV crews? Victoria kept asking. *Where are the TV crews?*

She had told all her friends that all the TV stations were coming. And it was our fault. Margie and Kristin, from our office, had made the worst possible mistake in our business. They promised her television. But because of their unpredictability, you never NEVER promise a client television. Or Louie Prima. Never tell a client that either is coming. No matter what the TV assignment desk editor says or promises, things happen along the way, especially when it's such a long way out in the boonies, like *Churchill's*. If they make it, great! It's a wonderful surprise. But to have someone like Victoria expecting television crews can be a fatal mistake. And it was. TV never showed. And she never forgave us. It's not like we didn't try to make amends. As *Churchill's* was a cigar-friendly restaurant, we took photographs of her puffing seductively on a cigar in front of her original painting of Sir Winston for *Cigar Aficionado* magazine.

We got *Nation's Restaurant Business* to run her picture and a story about *Churchill's*. We got all the local papers and glossy magazines to do splendid features on *Churchill's* opening. We portrayed it as the culmination of her many years of traveling throughout England and collecting four container loads of genuine English artifacts with which she painstakingly decorated the place.

The press reports acknowledged she had indeed created an authentic British dining experience. *I want my patrons to pinch themselves as they're leaving.* But for not getting those TV crews out to Cooper City, we were the ones who got pinched upon leaving. When our contract expired, she declined to renew. And we weren't that unhappy about it. At least we're getting some uninterrupted sleep at night.

30

The Game Endangered Species Want You To Play!

Who is known as the father of the Sea Grant College program? A) Albert Manville II; B) Bostwick Ketchem; C) Claiborne Pell; D) Michael Heiz; E) Thor Heyerdahl Hopefully by the time you're reading this, there's a board game in your closet or toy chest called *ENVIROCHALLENGE*.

It came with a *Certificate of Appreciation* that you're environmentally sensitive. *Hopefully* you've had it framed and mounted on your wall. And the bumper sticker that also was included is on your car helping to spread the word in your community. And *hopefully* you'll already have had fun playing *Envirochallenge*—more fun than you've ever had playing *Trivial Pursuit* or *Monopoly*. And you'll know that the father of the Sea Grant College is Claiborne Pell. And that in the past ten years, the portion of river water suitable for drinking in Poland has dropped from 32 percent to less than five percent. And due to transformation, nearly every molecule of water present when the seas were formed is still present today.

If you knew all this, then congratulations! You're a friend of the environment and part of the proceeds from your purchase of *Envirochallenge* has been passed on to an environmental organization dedicated to protecting the creatures and plant life we share our planet with. And I say all this *hopefully* because it's too early to tell whether this product we're promoting is going to be fruitful and multiply or become itself an endangered species!

After six months of meager and disappointing results, I wrote a letter to the Board of Directors of Global Horizons, Inc., urging them to *stay the course* for 90 more days:

> *We wish to assure you that we believe that significant media exposure for Envirochallenge is just ahead, including major print and television placements, which unfortunately have taken longer than we all expected to materialize. Because we believe that you are interested in results and not excuses, we will not dwell on the reasons that have delayed the media exposure we're all seeking for one of the most brilliant and important board games ever invented.*

When Mike Kashouty walked into our office with the idea nine months prior, it sounded exciting. Though he didn't have the prototype to show us yet, he convinced us that it's a game that would be fun to play, yet instructive about what we can do to save our planet. The pieces that move around the board were miniature endangered species: a whale, elephant, rhinoceros, wolf, sea turtle and a gorilla. The objective is to pursue, occupy and hold the *Office of the International Secretary of the Environment.* On each roll of the dice, players advance their token representing an endangered species and upon landing on certain blocks, must answer questions about the environment, resulting in rewards or penalities. The most challenging thing about *Envirochallenge*, however, is its price point: $59.95 plus $4.95 for shipping and handling.

Mike is a wide-eyed, soft-spoken inventor in his mid-forties. We don't know a great deal about him, except he seems very fond of black. Whenever we see him, he's wearing a black silk open-neck sport shirt that matches the nose guard on his tinted glasses. He removes those glasses occasionally to rub his eyes, which gives you the impression he could stand an hour or two more sleep at night. And Connie, his blonde associate, wears black skirts and knee-high leather boots.

Mike's energy comes in spurts, but his ideas flow from a seemingly inexhaustible supply of imagination, mixed with a rock-solid determination to make them work. Among his recent projects is a video on *How To Save Your Dog's Life*. If you think that's a silly topic, then answer me this: What would you do if you saw a Chihuahua choking on an onion ring? But like most entrepreneurs who launch products, Mike's ran into a storm of problems trying to get this one off mother earth. It has taken twice as long as he figured for the manufacturer to deliver the first 40,000 units. The endangered species miniatures weren't made just right, so they had to be sent back to China. And the most surprising difficulty of all, we've had trouble finding environmental groups willing to accept $2 for every game sold. We wanted to distribute the proceeds among several groups, representing a broad spectrum of environmental concerns.

But *Greenpeace* refused to grant us permission to use their name if the *Sierra Club* was involved. We didn't ask for endorsements, only the right to say that part of the proceeds were going to support their causes. But these environmental groups are jealous of each other. They're like spoiled children. Because they see the environment from only their particular vantage point, they'll accept your money, but not if you name different groups that you're also supporting. And they're wary when the commercial world comes calling. Down deep they believe it's the capitalists who pollute and muck up this world. And they wanted control over the questions, which was something Mike wasn't willing to do. And around it went.

It was environmentally screwy. Petty stuff. But Mike muddled through it. We hooked up Mike synergistically with Communications Service Centers, the best little calling center in the whole wide world and a client of ours. *Isn't there anybody in Florida who's not your client?* people ask me. But the truth is nobody's better at answering inbound toll-free calls than Herman Shooster, a fellow alumni of Temple University, his lovely wife Dorothy, their vivacious daughter Wendy, their three intelligent sons and their wonderful spouses and 400 alert operators using their proprietary state-of-the-art touch-screen technology at their sprawling center in Margate, Florida. Excuse my buttering up the Shoosters, but I'd like them to remain clients for at least a couple more generations.

And though we got the game written up in hundreds of newspapers, unveiled at the *Rain Forest Cafe*, infomercialized ad infinitum on TV and featured in full page ads in weekly newspapers and shoppers in the New York area, for the most part, Mike missed the 1996 Christmas selling season. Meanwhile, we're planning contests. Giving the game to science teachers. And getting Vice President Al Gore and his family to play it. Our plan is to harness the most powerful medium on earth—world-of-mouth—to propel *Envirochallenge* to your coffee table. If our booster rocket has failed so far to ignite you, then please, will somebody buy this game?

If you do, you can help to save the world and endangered species like this poor PR Man before you. By ordering your own *Envirochallenge* today, you can help us to hang on to an endangered account. Call toll free 888-978-8800 or order your *Envirochallenge* through the Internet: www.envirochallenge.com. If you won't do it for me, do it for the wolf.

Or the turtle?

Or the gipper.

Hell, I'll do anything to make a sale. Even in my memoirs.

31

The Icy Cold Vodka War

Would you call your approach toward me typical of the local morale?
Mademoiselle, it is that approach that has made Paris what it is.
I have heard of the arrogant male in capitalistic society.
A Russian! I love Russians.
It is having a superior earning power that makes you that way.

–Greta Garbo & Melvyn Douglas in *NINOTCHKA*

While things were going better with CocaCola in 1996, they had gone in the opposite direction for PepsiCo, one of the top 25 companies of the FORTUNE 500. Pepsi was badly wounded in the cola wars. Red ink was bleeding from its balance sheet. Casualties were high. According to *FORTUNE* magazine, in the summer and fall of 1996, Pepsi lost customers to Coke in every foreign territory. The company had always struggled overseas, but now it had lost key strongholds to Coke in Venezuela and in Russia. Even on the home front, Pepsi was outgunned. Coke's market share lead in the U.S. was the largest in 20 years. That was the scene when PepsiCo's brash Roger Enrico took over the job of CEO on April Fool's Day in 1996. He and his lieutenants were in the battle of their life against Coca-Cola's cerebrally-advantaged chairman, Roberto Goizueta.

But Enrico, the ultimate Cola warrior who wrote the 1986 book *The Other Guys Blinked: How Pepsi Won the Cola Wars*, had Coke in his cross hairs again. You'd think by now that a captain of industry like Enrico had learned from history about the folly of fighting multi-front wars. But not him. Not PepsiCo.

As if they didn't have enough trouble on their hands, they had to attack one of our clients, which brought me into the war on the side of Frank Pesce. Frank is a street-smart guy who bears a strong resemblance to Mike Wallace of *60 Minutes*. He speaks with a Brooklyn accent and it's not easy to make him blink.

The first thing I did was arm Frank with a slingshot, which I made out of twigs. I told him to keep it—along with a 16-ounce bottle of Pepsi—on his desk when he does press interviews. The slingshot was to symbolize Frank as David fighting PepsiCo as Goliath, which was no exaggeration. I called Kevin Gale, the business editor of the *Sun-Sentinel* and told him about the story.

It's a David and Goliath story, huh? Kevin asked.
You got it, Kevin. I'll send you a sling shot.

The giant PepsiCo has done everything to blitzkrieg over Pesce and his two daughters, Donna and Debbie. Together they constitute Frank Pesce Ltd., a tiny importer of Russian vodka located in Boca Raton, Florida. And they have proved to be as formidable an opponent to Enrico as Ethiopia was to El Duce. When PepsiCo called out Frank, they picked on the wrong guy. Frank's much tougher than they figured. He started out as a laborer and rose to builder and there's an aura about them that he can take care of himself. PepsiCo's strategy was to overwhelm him finan- cially. They had the typical Goliath mentality: *Who's this little punk dar- ing to fight us?* So they set out to *run the little guy ragged* and carbonate his life with problems and stumbling blocks of expensive litigation and injunctions. And they succeeded in preventing Pesce's little company from earning any revenue for a couple years. But that just made Frank mad and more determined. So the PepsiCo's strategy backfired.

Like all wars, this one has not been pretty. There were threats, attempted bribes and a brutal beating inflicted on Pesce's loyal Russian friend, Vladimir Jamnikov. It was intended to intimidate and force Pesce into giving up. But neither Frank nor Vladimir would budge, nor even blink. PepsiCo tried everything to break up a relationship between Pesce and Jamnikov, the director of the Moscow Distillery Cristall, that was set in reinforced concrete. *They must wonder what's holding these guys up? They tried everything to bring me to my knees.* So what was it that held David up and propelled him to fight on against Goliath? Why did Frank take such a risk and endure such a personal financial hardship? The answer is not one that's so easy to understand in today's mistrustful, litigious society. It was because of a friendship.

It used to be people would give their word, Frank says. *Today you shake hands and count your fingers.* But to Frank and Vladimir, their word still meant everything. And the friendship between a stubborn American and a just-as-stubborn Russian could not be broken. While Frank was raised in Brooklyn, Vladimir grew up under Communism, but, like his fellow countrymen, he had taken his first small steps toward capitalism and had become the director of a once state-owned distillery, now privatized under Russia's fledgling free-enterprise system. To understand their war with PepsiCo you have to look back into history. The scene is Russia during the height of the cold war. PepsiCo somehow strikes an historic deal with the government of that time, the Soviet Union. It was a remarkable achievement in a time when the U.S. placed a restriction on all American businesses from doing business with the USSR.

But somehow PepsiCo pulled it off. The Soviet Union agreed to buy the quintessential American product, PepsiCola, for sale to its citizens. Lacking sufficient hard currency, the Soviets agreed to pay PepsiCo in the form of a quintessential Russian product—vodka. It was through this classic barter arrangement—Pepsi for vodka—that PepsiCo became responsible for importing and distributing *Stolichnaya* vodka in the U.S., perhaps the most famous Russian product ever to be sold in the U.S. For years, *Stoli*, as it became known, was the only imported Russian vodka on the American market.

In the Soviet Union, the vodka industry, like all others, had been run by the Communist State. The State owned the distilleries. Its central economy decided which distilleries would make which vodkas, and where the vodkas would be exported. Vodka in Russia was a national treasure. The word *vodka* in Russian is a derivative of the Russian word for *water*. Even today, despite anti- alcohol campaigns, it is said that the average Russian male consumes about eight vodka drinks per day.

There was only one vodka distillery in the capital city of Moscow. And that was the Moscow Distillery Cristall. The distillery's stately brick walls and ornate, but unkempt, decor betrayed its age. It was founded in 1901 and was the most prestigious and oldest of Russia's 150 state distilleries. It was also the distillery responsible for exporting most of the *Stolichnaya* vodka to PepsiCo for U.S. distribution. Around 1988, PepsiCo, having lost a large market share of *Stolichnaya* vodka to *Absolut* from Sweden, became interested in importing a second, premium brand of vodka from the Soviet Union. So in early 1989, Stolichnaya Cristall was introduced in the U.S. as a top-of-the-line vodka. It received rave reviews. *It is certainly the Chateau Lafite-Rothschild of vodkas*, wrote Anthony Dias Blue in the February 1990 issue of *Bon Appetit*. Initial shipments sold out in months and the brand became a smashing success.

Then turmoil in the Soviet Union led to the privatization of industry and the dissolution of the Soviet State on Christmas Day, 1991. In the process, the Moscow Distillery Cristall became a private company with Jamnikov its director. By then PepsiCo had already embarked on a scheme to sell counterfeit vodka in bottles labeled *Stolichnaya Cristall*. The scheme would last to 1994 and in the process PepsiCo would try to steal the Cristall trademark. This was the heart of our media story that we took to *The Wall Street Journal*, *BusinessWeek* and *60 Minutes*.

The Moscow Distillery Cristall had a practice of stamping a factory code imprint in the back of each label of *Stolichnaya Cristall*. The stamp's code number identified the distillery and the date of production of each bottle of vodka. The code enables the distillery to track any bottle of vodka which might be adulterated or otherwise be defective. Around May of 1993, PepsiCo directed the distillery to stop putting the stamp on the back of the labels. It was an odd request. The reason given was that the stamp was damaging the labels. But in fact, it was the first of three steps in PepsiCo's scheme of deception. Innocently, the distillery went along with PepsiCo's request. And in late 1993, PepsiCo embarked on the second step of the scheme. PepsiCo made a secret deal with another distillery in St. Petersburg, Russia, to make another vodka and sell it as *Stolichnaya Cristall*. And then the final step.

PepsiCo altered the text of the Stoli Cristall labels, but ever so slightly, so as to be unnoticeable to the unsuspecting eye. Where the original label stated *From the Cristall Distillery in Moscow comes the rarest and finest Russian vodka*, the altered label stated *From the Celebrated Grand Distilleries of Russia comes the rarest and finest Russian vodka*. PepsiCo supplied the St. Petersburg distillery with these new labels to apply to the bottles of the substitute vodka.

Then through their exclusive distributors, Carillon Importers, Ltd. Of Teaneck, New Jersey, PepsiCo began importing and selling in the U.S. the counterfeit vodka labeled *Stolichnaya Cristall*, which, because of the absence of any factory code was completely impossible to trace back to the source. The scheme, said Moscow Distillery Cristall's lawyers, was just like selling Pepsi in a Coca-Cola can.

Now it happened around midway into PepsiCo's scheme in 1992 that Pesce traveled to Moscow with a group interested in redeveloping a portion of downtown Moscow. Pesce took a tour of the Moscow Distillery Cristall and there Pesce met Jamnikov and struck up an immediate friendship with the small, quiet Russian.

Both men had much in common. Their belief in family, trust and loyalty. And both are stubbornly alike in their adamant refusal to give in and surrender what they know is their property. That property is the world's most valuable trademark in vodka—Cristall. Since neither spoke the other's language, the bond that developed between Pesce and Jamnikov was truly remarkable.

When we talk, there's an interpreter, but we look at each other and communicate with our eyes. I would die for this man and I'm certain he would do the same for me, affirms Pesce.

It was Pesce who first discovered the PepsiCo scam. He immediately contacted his friend Jamnikov. Infuriated, Jamnikov refused to sell any more Stolichnaya Cristall to PepsiCo and gave importation rights to his trusted associate Pesce. And Jamnikov directed that Pesce bring a lawsuit against PepsiCo on behalf of the Moscow Distillery Cristall. In early 1995, the distillery, represented by Pesce, initiated a lawsuit in Federal Court in Seattle, Washington.

It was a bold move for a small Russian company to take on an America icon in a U.S. court. Like soldiers sharing a foxhole, Pesce and Jamnikov were now drawn closer than ever before. They were fiercely loyal to one another, dependent on each other and committed to a struggle against a powerful adversary. After three weeks of testimony and over a week of deliberations, the jury unanimously found that Moscow Distillery Cristall owned the *Cristall* trademark and that PepsiCo illegally infringed on the distillery's trademark by selling substitute vodka from another distillery under the *Cristall* name. The jury also found from the evidence that PepsiCo's conduct was *willful* in that it was *calculated to exploit the good will* of the Moscow Distillery Cristall's established mark or *by an intention to deceive.* The verdict was a landmark decision because it is the first known instance since the post-communist era where a Russian company has taken on a major U.S. company and won. There were press reports about it all over the world.

For a fledgling enterprise like Moscow Distillery Cristall trying to make its way under the new free enterprise system, it was a great victory. At stake were not only many millions of dollars, but the respective survival of two small businesses. One American. The other Russian. The Federal judge in Seattle issued an injunction to stop PepsiCo from selling its counterfeit Cristall. And because the jury had found PepsiCo's deceptive practices were *willful,* it trebled the damages to nearly $3 million for Pesce and the Moscow Distillery Cristall. While PepsiCo's underhanded tactics would cause Russians to be wary of the sharp and sometimes illegal business practices of even the largest American companies, the vindication brought by the jury's verdict also brought renewed faith in the American system. Jamnikov had traveled halfway around the world to tell his story and to seek justice in an American courtroom against an American icon. And that justice was rendered. That a jury of ordinary citizens was able to put aside years of cold war prejudice tells us something good about our system. And Davids like Frank Pesce are a joy to know and a privilege to represent.

32

Here is the gist of a practical list of don'ts for you.
—Oklahoma!

D on't Throw Bouquets or Laugh At Your Client's Jokes Too Much. They'll respect you more when you tell them they're dead wrong or they're about to make an ass of themselves. I've gotten much more mileage out of frightening than flattering. Fear gets their attention.

Don't Go Into Business With a Media Person! In public relations, you could say we're surrogates for the media. Their assistants even. Certainly we represent our clients first and foremost, but we're obligated to help the media, too, in terms of providing accurate information and reasonable perspective.

You soon learn in this business that if you hype too much, you're going to lose your credibility. A PR person without credibility with the press is like a lawyer mistrusted by judges. If the media don't believe you, how are you going to serve your clients? At the same time, you want to cultivate friendships with people in the media because that can be your stock in trade. I've made lots of money over the years just mentioning reporters I know. But why risk those valuable friendships by going into business? I used to be great friends with Dan Dorfman, for example, until I created a television series in the 1980s expressly for this raspy-throated reporter and commentator on CNBC. The property was a spoof on investing called *I Dream of Money*. I thought I could make a financial show funny, but I was wrong. Our jokes about Wall Street flopped like a bear market. We produced two pilot episodes in front of a live audience. They were paid for by Lesta Stacum, the wife of the Chairman of the large real estate firm, Cushman & Wakefield. I was the producer; Lesta the investor. What I lost was time, energy and my entre with Dorfman. Lesta lost about $35,000. And to this day, we have not spoken. Try telling people who've lost money on your ideas that you tried your best. It won't change the way they feel. So all I can say is *Sorry Dan. Sorry Lesta.*

Why Isn't There A TV In Every Bathroom?

While I'm at it, I want also to apologize to Albert Timsit, a Moroccan-born immigrant with a booming voice and hearty laugh who led the Moroccan Jewish community in New York City. Albert gave me $50,000 to start *Video Newscasting Network*, a television industry trade magazine on videotape, which I created, produced and hosted and persuaded former FCC Chairman Mark Fowler to be my co-host. Poor Albert was hardly a passive investor. He worked harder than I've ever seen anyone work trying to sell commercial time on our videos to Paramount Television and other program distributors who wanted to reach buyers at local stations. Meanwhile, I was being interviewed by *Forbes* and *TIME* magazine and hailed as an innovator.

TIME quoted me saying *I couldn't understand why television wasn't using its own medium to circulate industry news*. It wasn't until after we produced a dozen hour-long programs, delivered on videotape cassette to about 500 television station executive subscribers across the country, did it become apparent why broadcasters prefer their news in print. One obviously constipated program manager put it this way: *You can't take a VCR into the bathroom with you*. We tried to raise more money, but interest rates had shot up. We slogged along for a year, but couldn't turn a profit. Meanwhile Albert's investment had gone down the toilet. Frustrated and exhausted, we decided to throw up our hands. I returned to PR, while Albert divorced his wife and moved to Jerusalem. He remarried and started a restaurant there, which I heard he later sold. Entrepreneurship can be hazardous to your personal life. And it can cost a lot of innocent people their shekels. Unfortunately my good-spirited and brave Moroccan friend Albert had to be one of them.

<u>Don't promise clients a damn thing.</u> Since we have no control over media, the best policy is to avoid guaranteeing or promising any results. I tell clients not to expect any tangible results in terms of meaningful exposure for 60 to 90 days and even then there's no guarantee we'll be effective. The only thing we should promise is our best efforts. PR people always get themselves in trouble when client expectations get too far ahead of realistic probabilities.

33

Some Short Spins

Over the years I've put quite a few spins on things. Before I summarize just a few of the more noteworthy, you might be interested in the thought process that goes into a public relations campaign. Let's start with an entrepreneur who just launched a chain of discount stores. He has opened three stores in the past year, but he's disappointed because there hasn't been a word about them in the press, even though they're all doing quite well featuring generic products, which he is selling for at least 50 percent below what comparable store brands cost at the large chain drugstores. The problem is how do we make his stores seem dramatically new and different?

Lots of times I'll begin a campaign by writing what I believe is an effective news release that will interest the press. Then we'll reconstruct reality to conform to what's written in the release, essentially turning it into a sort of script for the program. For example, in featuring side-by-side price comparison of generic products with more expensive name brands with virtually identical ingredients, here's an entrepreneur appealing to the educated consumer. He's basically saying that people who buy his generic equivalents are: *Smart. Informed. Educated!* These are the key ideas. So how do we emphasize them? One of the ways is to position our entrepreneur client, Jerry Rayman, as a genius in retailing generic products and someone helping consumers to achieve huge savings when they shop at his C$C Discount Stores, which we rename C$C *SmartMart*. We introduce visuals or props that underscore this fact, like having checkers wear college graduation caps with tassels as a salute to educated shoppers. We issue diplomas to customers verifying they are smart consumers and create an *Ollie the Owl* character to make appearances at Senior Centers and lead bus loads of seniors to SmartMarts for Senior Savings Days. And here's the news release, or script, I wrote before we purchased our first tassel.

> **FOR IMMEDIATE RELEASE**
> **DEERFIELD BEACH, FL., Jan. 6, 1997.**—*Practically everything Jerry Rayman does is smart. Some even call him a "generic guru."*
>
> *His C$C Discount Stores are the only super discount drugstores in America where you'll find checkers wearing graduation caps with tassels as "a salute to educated consumers." And where shoppers receive diplomas.*
>
> *A true generic entrepreneur, he constantly reminds today's value-conscious shoppers that they're smart for selecting generic products over name brands at his rapidly-growing chain of C$C Discount Stores, which opened in South Florida only a year ago.*
>
> *Intent on building a national chain, he is intelligently pioneering his concept in Florida of displaying generic equivalents alongside their name brand counterparts, emphasizing that consumers need only pay a fraction of the price for virtually identical ingredients. According to the generic guru, that translates into big savings for those "smart enough to shop at C$C."*

Another example involves the *Acura Legend*. The owner of an Acura store tells us he wants more people to appreciate his dealership. We think it would elevate his image if he associated with the arts. So we propose he sponsor one of the region's top ballet companies and art museums. By doing so, we'll underscore *Acura: Where Selling Is An Art And The Car Is A Masterpiece.*

We explain how we'll exhibit art in his showroom. Drape pairs of ballet shoes on Acuras. Have an artist paint pictures of cars and then paint buyers into the pictures, which we'll frame and exhibit. Provide a scholarship for an inner-city child to attend the Miami Ballet School. But the dealer turns out to be a Philistine. He has little interest in art or museums, calls our program too high brow and runs us off the road. I'm still chafing over it when I bump into the regional director of marketing for Mercedes at the Miami Ballet. I tell him about our Acura fiasco and ask if he'd like to see our proposal which is more in harmony with the upscale Mercedes. He invites me to send it to him. If he doesn't like it, it goes to Jaguar. Word processors are like freeways. If one lane is blocked, you scoot around and take another.

Next involves a subject that's no joking matter. And that's exactly why we decided to use comedy to break the ice and relieve the tension surrounding *impotence,* so men might discuss it more openly. First thing I did was re-name the chain of impotency-treatment centers *Physicians Health & Diagnostics,* which gave it the catchier acronym *PHD.* Then to help communicate their message, I drew two penguins, one a male penguin in an orchestra who had just climactically clashed the symbols. Hugging him affectionately from behind is a pleased-looking Mrs. Penguin who says: *Honey, I just love how you perform.* Using comedy to set the stage for a touchy subject? We thought the press would find it unusual enough to write about. And we were right. We got media to cover seminars we held at retirement communities for our client. Here's an excerpt from a stand-up routine written by one of our account executives that we used to gather an audience, relieve tension and attract media exposure:

Actually, impotency is one of the biggest growth industries. It's true. And Physicians Health & Diagnostics is on the cutting edge. Wait a minute, let me find a better phrase, Physicians Health & Diagnostics is taking a firm hold of the situation, no that doesn't work either. Let's see.

Physicians Health & Diagnostics is reaching new heights, yeah that's better, with their proven successful methods to treat impotency.

Here's some of the theme songs we're considering for *PHD:*
1. "I'm Down" by the Beatles
2. "Up, Up and Away" by The Fifth Dimension.
3. "Is That All There Is" by Peggy Lee.

Now let me take you on a few quick spins from over the years:

- **Moving the mountain to Mohammed.** Invited high rollers to a private champagne party at Cartier's on Fifth Avenue in New York—ostensibly to preview Cartier's Paris Collection, but really to hear about a $200 million luxury condominium we were promoting in Atlantic City. A five-column headline in *The Philadelphia Inquirer* summed it up well: *Quietly and elegantly they're selling ocean-view luxury.*

- **What's in a name? Plenty!** Induced media in the Northeast to adopt the title I created for Joe Murphy, president of Drexel Burnham Lambert Real Estate. Joe had raised a billion dollars to build three casinos and a condo in Atlantic City. I dubbed him *The Financial Helmsman of Atlantic City.* And the name stuck to Joe like money did during that golden era of junk bonds. He was so happy with results, he let me publicize a million-dollar gift he gave to his alma mater Iona College, where I got to meet the Dalai Lama, who spoke there one day. No, I did not say *Hello Dalai.*

- **Talk about a picture-perfect takeoff.** Unveiled *Picturephone Meeting Service,* AT&T's new visual teleconferencing network and got Academy of Motion Picture Arts & Sciences President Fay Kanin to make the inaugural call from LA to simultaneous news conferences in New York, Pittsburgh and Washington, D.C., all linked by satellite so everyone could see everyone else. The kickoff was sensational. The pictures were clear. The service was a bust. Apparently few companies wanted PMS.

- **Mission over France.** Had airplanes pull banners over the Cannes Film Festival inviting the industry to *The Florida Riviera*—Fort Lauderdale. And dropped stacks of Sherry Friedlander's *Business In Broward* magazines off on every floor of the Carlton Hotel. The grunt work struck a masochistic funny bone. *Beat me, beat me,* I told the publisher who has a fetish for giving PR people hernias. The herculean effort motivated more than 200 film buyers from 24 countries and over a 100 film companies to participate in the Fort Lauderdale International Film Market. Also, my friend Prof. Richard Brown, host of AMC's *Reflections on a Silver Screen,* helped me get some extra publicity for the film festival by creating *The Frank Capra Award* for Academy-Award-winning actor Van Johnson in 1991. That same year we gave lifetime achievement awards to Burt Reynolds, Donald O'Connor and Jerry Lewis in a program that ran longer than *The Nutty Professor.*

- **A whole new call game!** Got KFMB to be the first radio station to cover a World Series using cellular phones. AT&T's Burke Stinson and I also gave some of the first *live* radio interviews in Manhattan from a *car phone.* Afraid of losing our signal in the cavernous city, we did the interviews while parked in an elevated, remote spot near a cell site north of the George Washington Bridge. Pretending to be cruising around Manhattan, Burke added in descriptive tidbits like *we're just passing Carnegie Hall now* as I honked the horn to simulate driving in city traffic. A few years later, Burke rose to become the chief press spokesman for AT&T. But every once in a while, we'll reflect on those early makeshift days. I still wonder what joggers and bicyclists must have thought that day seeing two grown men in business suits sitting in a parked car practicing horn honking. With portables so common-place today, the scene probably makes me sound old as Methuselah, but it was only in the mid 80s when cellular phones were still in the gee-whiz category. And we racked up quite a lot of publicity mileage with them for AT&T.

- **It's a bird. It's a plane. It's the mayor!** Stimulated a record number of calls to New York City's Fair Housing Hotline by teaming up Mayor Ed Koch and TV tough-guy Mr. T as crusaders against discrimination in housing. Arranged a news conference for the super heroes at the taping of PSA spots directed by Bob Giraldi. And won a Bronze Anvil from PRSA for the pro bono project.

- **Colorful cocktails.** Promoting "Painting With Elke Sommer," a new PBS series, we had Elke *mix acrylics* behind the bar at Antolotti's Restaurant in New York, teach Regis Philbin how to paint on his TV show and pose for photographers beside vats of paint at Grumbacher's plant in Manhattan. And had her accept a "Boehm Bird" sculpture from Helen Boehm, unaware at the time that Mrs. Boehm gave her birds to practically every celebrity. I later worked with chutzpa Helen on a some charity affairs in Palm Beach.

- **Viva La Shtick.** For a carpet cleaning company called Magi-Kiss, created *CHICAGO'S MOST KISSABLE LIPS CONTEST* and got thousands of female entrants to pucker up and plant one on a postcard postmarked S.W.A.K., which was mailed in to the company for judging. It received such a smooch in *USA TODAY*, we were asked to come up with a promotion for Buzet, a new French wine. We came up with a nationwide search for the best look-ing woman in a beret, whom we crowned *MISS BUZET BERET*! She wore her cute little beret on just about every TV station in New York City. (I'm now doing penance for all these sexist promotions.)

All this immodesty inspires me to tell one of my favorite stories about a woman who goes to see her OBGYN. After examining her, he's astonished to find she's still a virgin. Knowing she's been married several times, he couldn't help asking how this was possible.

"You're still a virgin?"

"Yes, I am, Doctor."

"But you've been married three times, haven't you?"

"Yes, my first was to a man who was to inherit a great deal of money on his wedding day. So it was just a marriage of convenience."

"And the second husband?"

"That was a sad situation. I married a veteran who was severely wounded in the worst of all places. So our marriage was never consummated."

"What about your current husband? He looks pretty healthy."

"Yes. But he's in public relations. When we go to bed at night, all he ever does is go to the end of the bed, rub my legs and tell me how good it's going to be." (Rim Shot)

34

Unwinding From Spinning

Every once in a while in our office, you'll hear shrieking, whooping and hollering, hand clapping and desk pounding emanating from the office of one of our account executives. You might even see one of them run out into the hallway, jump up and down and yell YES! YES! YES! We love when that happens. It's the exciting sound of success in our business. It means someone just got a *hit*. A media score. A placement! They've just *placed* one of our clients on a national show. Or got a major magazine or newspaper hit. An editor interested. A reporter hooked. And they're celebrating like African natives do after they spear a lion. Only our lions and tigers are producers and editors. And I can't tell you how exhilarating it feels to spear one.

The life of a spin man is full of topspin and excitement. By stimulating even just one major article or appearance on a network show, there's no telling how profoundly it will affect a client's fortunes, not to mention your own, if you own stock in the company. So it's constant tension, relieved by moments of joy. PR firms are like hospital emergency rooms. Clients call you in cardiac arrest. *Our stock is sinking. Please do something. Get a release out.* So we rush the patient into surgery. Find something we can operate on. And get it out fast. Hopefully *Dow Jones News Wire* will pick it up. If so, the patient's heart will revive. The account will be saved. A disaster averted. But from so much excitement every day, one needs a change of pace. Mine is running on the beach three times a week. Call it jogging. Slogging maybe? Okay schlepping. But how I hate it when one of those fancy-ass-swishing-walkers passes me. Oh how I hate that!

After running about three miles, I stop for breakfast at the *Dune Deck Cafe* on the beach next to the Ritz-Carlton. Do I get the wait-ress who won the ice cream company's *hot legs* contest? No, I get the blonde crowned *Miss Nursing Home*. And she asks me gratingly if I had a good *walk*. At least once a week, I remind her that I *run. I don't walk. I run! It might look like I'm walking, but I'm RUNNING. It's definitely a jog. Not a walk.* And I think to myself: what idiot can't see I'm a runner. Look at me. How perspired I am. You don't get a workout like that from walking. *No, I'm no walker. I'm a run-ner.* She smiles patronizingly, hands me the menu that I can recite blindfolded. *I don't need this. I know about the tropical fruit cup and the pancakes with fresh strawberries. I eat breakfast here three times a week after my run.* Unfazed, she asks in that saccharin, nurs-ing-home-terminal-bedpan tone of hers: *And what would we like for breakfast this morning? Eggs over runny,* I answer. *How's that? Runny! I like the yellow to run like I do. Let'em run all over the plate right into the home fries.* I have to keep reminding myself that she's not trying to irritate me. She can't help herself. It's because Florida has such a huge proportion of older folks, waitresses have been conditioned to talking down to their customers as if they're all senile, hard of hearing, brain dead zombies in dire need of cutesy-wootzy cheering up. To them, the state symbol might as well be a cane or walker. So sitting there alone, perspiring from a long, hard run, I give her *our* order.

Go West Young Man To The Country Club

All of the golf courses in our area are west of us. So I advise PR people to go west and play golf. I don't. The ball's too small. (Rim shot.) And because of it, I've lost accounts to competitors. Oh I have a 500-pound Ben Hogan bag full of clubs, all right. They never go anywhere, though. One of these days, I'm going to learn. For a spin man who wants to meet clients, avoiding the links is a definite handicap. They say if you want to bag a moose, you have to go where the moose are. And the moose are all out there hacking away on golf courses.

One of my favorite pastimes is reclining on the couch and watching one of our favorite clients score touchdowns. He's veteran wide receiver Irving Fryar, a first-round draft pick a dozen years ago when he started with New England. Since then, Irving has had his ups and downs, both personally and professionally. No matter how rough it gets, however, he never loses his springy step or engaging sense of humor. And he always greets us with a warm hug and a grin wide enough to disarm a street gang. But he's so damn trim and muscular, I hate to stand next to him. He has one of the lowest proportions of body fat in the NFL.

On a pedestal in our living room sits an encased autographed football he gave us for helping him to find a free home for his foundation to help disadvantaged children. And we arrange speaking engagements for him to talk about it. He's a preacher. And, praise Jesus, can he ever talk! And talk. There's a lot bottled up inside of him which is spellbinding when it comes out. He cares deeply about kids. And a father's responsibility. *You women do a pretty fair job, but kids need the man. But to grow up straight and tall, they need THE MAN! They need a father AT HOME!* But too many are deserters. He'll tell you that one out of every four American babies are born to unmarried women. That vanishing fathers is an epidemic. And he knows first hand the temptations. About drugs. Fast cars. He's totaled a few himself. And women who go gaga around him. But he's devoted to his beautiful wife, Jackie, and their children. And to his church and teammates. When *The Miami Dolphins* failed to pick up his contract for the '96 season, he went to play for *The Philadelphia Eagles*. In his first game against the *Dolphins* in Miami, he burned them with four TD receptions. Go Irving! You're the man!

A Good Vowel Movement

Writing is the backbone of PR. Everything begins with the printed word. A client begins with the printed word. You usually don't get paid until you create and deliver a proposal to someone, a written blue print of what you're going to do for them, what methods you intend to employ, what objectives you expect to accomplish, topped off with how long you think it's going to take and what it's going to cost. And the culmination of any program is the *news release*. How well it's written and what it conveys often determine if a program will be successful. Often we'll write the news release in our minds first and then construct a program that will live up to it.

So writing ability is one of the main things I always look for when hiring a publicist. If I'm not sure, I'll give someone a writing test. Put them at a word processor and see if they can whip up a snappy release in 30 minutes. One of the best writers on our staff is actually a produced playwright. Richard Harlowe came to us with a one of the most diverse backgrounds I've ever encountered. His resume read like an oxymoron. He was a fact checker at a tabloid. An insurance salesman who wrote plays. When I first asked him about writing, he told me he had *good vowel movement*. And I hired him on the spot.

DOS For Dummies

It wasn't too long ago when people tentatively asked if you had a fax machine. And then you became a Neanderthal if you didn't have at least one. Today, people request your E-mail address as perfunctorily and airline ticket counter personnel ask for your ID. And you'd better have a web site or an arresting home page on the Internet or a platoon of bit heads will march your image up against a blank screen and click — one more dinosaur deleted. Incidentally, some of the smartest people I know are technological idiots. Yet their screen is a whole lot wider than 15 inches. So don't mistake them for dummies. And the medium reaching 100 percent of the population of the world is not the Internet. It's still the all powerful postcard. And handwritten!

Keeping Impatient Clients In Line

Tell the client it has taken longer than expected to achieve the results you've been promising. Explain that the one aspect of PR you can't accurately predict is *when* an exposure is going to occur because that's a factor of the media's agenda, over which you have little control. Get clients to think of it this way. We've all waited in lines. This is no different. The press has the information. They've indicated they'll do something. So we're almost at the window. If you replace us with another firm, they'll only have to start at the rear of the line.

What's A Fair Fee?

The public relations fee has always been an enigma. And that's as it should be. Let's not get too mathematical about it. Many firms bill by the hour and submit detailed time sheets to clients ostensibly showing how much time was spent on their behalf. But that begs the question: Does time equal effort? Or results? I prefer charging a flat retainer fee corresponding to the magnitude of the program or project.

Over time I believe it's a fairer system. It's results oriented, not effort oriented. Sometimes it will take weeks of work to achieve results. Then there have been times when I have completely satisfied and impressed a client after only a two-minute phone call resulting in a major media placement. But look how many years it has taken me to learn how to make that call, to know the person on the other end, to know what to say and how to speak his or her language.

Thou Shalt Level With Thy Clients

Only fools and scam artists are brazen enough to promise swift results. No matter how well connected you are, or from how high a mount you deliver your sermon, if you promise a client easy or quick results, you're only asking for trouble. It usually takes longer than anyone believes. For

2,000 years Jesus of Nazareth has been sending out His message. And still it hasn't spread far enough nor, for the most part, has it sunken in.

What They're Wearing For Camouflage These Days

Enthusiasm is at the same time a PR person's weapon and camouflage. It's a super fuel that can drive action and convince a client that you're excited to represent them and you expect to be successful on their behalf. But it's a coat of many colors. While it delights and flatters, it might also cover deficiencies. So hire people who have it, but don't let it blind you to their shortcomings. I know PR people who wear enthusiasm like a bright pink badge on their lapels or shirt sleeves. Who parade around with it and pop it out in meetings. It's contagious and I welcome it. But it can cloak their ineptitude. I know PR people who can't write, who can't conceptualize, strategize, or manage anything more complicated than a handshake, but they're talented at being enthusiastic, at sitting at their clients' feet oozing with breathless interest in their every word. Watch for the telltale signs. If you hear them, be careful. The enthusiasm you're seeing and hearing may be a trick to get your fee.

Here are some suspicious phrases to look out for: *You did that? I've never heard anything so exciting in my life. Oh, was that ever a coup. You're so smart. How did you ever think of that? That's so amazing. What a wonderful story that is. We have to get that out to the press right away.* Many PR people I know make a living being enthusiastic. I don't necessarily knock it. We all do what we can to survive. And for some egocentric clients, it can be a soothing balm, a sweet kiss on their cheeks. And who knows, it might even accomplish something.

The 'I's' Don't Have It

If anyone is deranged enough to be attracted to the PR field from what I have written, please take a tip from someone who has received perhaps over 10,000 resumes throughout his career. The word is written in tiny type because that's about the impact most resumes have had on me. Don't send them unless accompanied by a <u>persuasive</u> cover letter. *Persuasive communications* is what PR is all about. Right off the bat you need to demonstrate your skill at being persuasive. And what I mean by that is you need to persuade a prospective employer that your focus is on him or her . . . on helping **me**, not **yourself**. Yet most transmittal letters are blatantly egocentric. Most job applicants **I** you to death. Most resume transmittal letters read something like this: **I** am a recent college graduate or I am an experienced publicist. And **I** have done this. And **I** can do that. And **I** would like to . . . **I** . . . **I** . . . **I** . . . **I** . . . But do you know what is the most powerful word in persuasive communications? The word is **you**! If you wish to make an impression on **me**, demonstrate that you've taken the time to learn something about **my** business. And about **me**. Tell me how you can help **me** to attract more clients or help **me** to serve them more effectively. How you can help **me** solve **my** problems and not just yours!

Yes We Have No Soliciting

There's a sign in our lobby that is quite blunt about it: *No Soliciting.* It avoids a lot of interruptions and maybe strange, even dangerous, people wandering around our building. But in a way I'm sorry not to see sales people who can smile and talk their way in to try to sell me something. No, please that's not an invitation. *I'm busy as hell. I don't need it. But what is it?*

Selling is one of those skills you can learn from anyone who is good at it. Or bad at it. When applicants tell me they've tried sales and didn't like it very much and now they're seeking a position in public relations, I listen politely, but my mind begins rummaging through the rest of my appointments for I know this one isn't going to pan out. Soon as I get a chance, I'll end the interview mercifully as I can. PR is sales. That's what it's all about. There's no escaping it. So if you're not into selling, stay out of our lobby. Not only is selling essential to survival, it's the most satisfying part of a spin man's day. The hunt. The scent. The signed contract. It gets into your blood. And belongs there. Like the other day when I went to see this young Brazilian black couple who had just bought *Justa Pasta,* a Coral Gables restaurant that had been closed for several months. They picked our toll-free number out of the Miami Yellow Pages.

Justa Pasta turned out to be a cute little place, but counting the tables and doing some quick math in my head, I knew they couldn't afford $5,000 a month or $3,000. But Joao Barros (pronounced "Jew-owl"), the owner, had a gleaming smile and an appetizing way about him. And I was impressed to learn that he had been a chef at some of the top restaurants in Paris. Locally he had cooked privately for Sly Stallone. And Madonna loved his avocado salad. So I wanted very much to sell him for I knew our publicity could help a lot. But I had to be careful about not concentrating just on him. I had to make his wife want our services too. For I know from my own experience that in most businesses there's usually one who's the banker/bookkeeper with both feet squarely on the ground, who balances and checks the visionary/dreamer/entrepreneur who's driving everybody nuts. So if I was to snare this account, I'd have to capture them both.

I proceeded to tell them about all the TV shows we could have Joao Barros cooking on . . . the celebrities we could bring in for dinner into a private room they needed to create. And to add Brazilian specialties to the menu and call the restaurant *Justa Pasta Plus*, because it would be more than pasta. It would be a touch of Brazil . . . a celebrity hang-out . . . and we'd make Joao Barros a famous chef who would appear on television shows, maybe Regis and Kathy Lee. And of course we'll have a grand opening and invite the press and restaurant reviewers and plus, plus, plus.

With every plus his eyes sparkled and his smile widened. When I quoted them a certain amount per month, he looked sheepishly at his wife, but she had folded her arms and was staring out the window into the sun-lit street as if that's where their money was to pay for this extravagant picture I was painting, out there wilting in the afternoon sun. I could see disappointment welling up in his eyes. *Isn't that a great idea what he said?* Joao Barros says to her. *He says we should make here a private room for celebrities. They could smoke cigars.* Her arms stayed folded. It was obvious his dreams of glory had crashed into those implacable folded arms. Discouraged, he turned to me. *That's a lot of money for us right now,* he said sadly. Then he uttered the words every sales person dreads hearing. *We'll think it over.*

No. They mustn't think it over. He's young, but not that young. The curtain must not close here or the play will be over for both of us. Someone else will sell them -- maybe a bill of goods. Not the real stuff I was offering. No, this hard-working couple needed our services. Without promotion and publicity, they'll work themselves sick and never make it big. And one day he'll put his spoons and ladles into a drawer, flop exhausted into a reclining chair and live maybe a month or two watching The Food Channel. The situation reminded me of my father and what he used to tell me. How he could play violin as well as Heifitz, but to make it big, you needed more than fine musicianship. You needed what all the great violinists had. Great promoters! If only I was a spin man then. I could have helped my talented father to the top. Instead of the Traymore Hotel in Atlantic City, New Jersey, maybe he could have played Carnegie Hall. He was a great violinist.

So I sat next to Joao Barros' wife, Rosalia. And applied every drop of salesmanship I could squeeze out of me at 4 PM on a Friday after a long drive and a spinning week of meetings, parties and bullshit. And I went to work on that stoic banker/bookkeeper staring blankly out the window. *I have an idea,* I said to her. *We can make this program not only more affordable, but have it start to bring in customers immediately.* She looked at me. I had struck the right chord. They needed business tomorrow, not next month, which was the soonest that publicity could break.

You can pay part of our monthly fee in food and beverage credit. And we'll use that credit to stimulate immediate business. Starting Monday I'll have someone bring new customers in for lunch and each day we'll work off that credit in a way that will fill this place. After someone eats for free, they will return with their friends. And those customers will beget other customers and business will multiply as we prepare the private room for celebrity dining. Lines will appear at the entrance. (I was thinking I could hire my cousin Richard Imperiale's wife, who worked in a nearby office building. It was perfect. Ginger was a Mary Kay distributor on the side. Wouldn't she love to take Mary Kay prospects out to lunch for free?) Rosalia's arms began unfolding. I whipped out the contract, repeating silently the salesperson's mantra: *get the order . . . get the order. Let's make our agreement for six months starting immediately.* Joao Barros and his wife agreed. And I drove back up to Boca as satisfied as if I had eaten a five-course dinner at the Four Seasons, topped off with a unique dessert: flambe of folded arms made of rich dark chocolate. Reader, if you're ever in Miami, you've got to try this wonderful little restaurant. Tell Joao Barros and Rosalia the spin man sent you.

35

Updates

Tova Comes Through!

Picture a penthouse way up in the sky. And put Tova Leidesdorf into it. She phones us out of the blue to ask if we would like to meet the King of Jordan. *The King? Saturday night? Sure. We'd love to.* She had bought a $10,000 table at *The David Ben-Gurion* University dinner at the Ritz-Carlton in Palm Beach and invited us to join her. She also wants us to meet her new boyfriend, Erwin Herling, a 75-year-old chemist with a Ph. D., who is also an industrial engineer, an inventor and an entrepreneur who had established the textile industry in Eastern Europe in the aftermath of destruction of World War II. Prior to the dinner, we drove down to see Tova and Erwin at his tri-plex penthouse at the Alexander Hotel in Miami Beach. And to our delight, we discover Erwin is much more than a colossal success. He is also a fine pianist, composer, poet, humorist, artist, art collector, magician and linguist who speaks 17 languages. He is also a survivor of the Auschwitz death camp.

> *It was a raw day in 1943. Herling was lined up with other Jews in front of a trench which they had just dug. In a few seconds, Nazi soldiers would open fire on them with machine guns and Herling and the other prisoners would fall into*

172

their self-made mass grave. But Erwin had a flash of inspira-
tion. Moments before the execution, he told one of the Nazi
guards it was his birthday. If only he could be spared just one
more day, he would gratefully submit to being shot the next
day. The guard listened to the pitiful plea in amazement for
the day before had been his own birthday and the day before
that had been the Fuhrer's birthday. With his rifle butt, he
knocked Erwin out of line. And our wonderful new friend
lived that day and managed to avoid being shot the next day
and the next until the camp was liberated.

Erwin immigrated to Brazil and in a few years managed to have 40 fac-
tories working for him behind the *Iron Curtain.* They turned out products
which he traded for other products, then traded again for still other products around the world. He says the only thing communists ever wanted
out of any deal was their cost back. *They were interested only in keeping*
people working. They could care less about making a profit. In the process,
they were leaving gold in the streets. I just went over and picked it up.

Recently he donated $25 million to Herzog Hospital in Jerusalem from
the great fortune he is said to have amassed. From the looks of his penthouse, you could tell he had a few shekels. It's the penultimate apartment! Spiral staircases lead you to one spectacular level after another.
Opulence abounds. On the top floor is a recreation of a Venetian scene.
Gold inlaid customized furniture from Paris and original oils uplift every
room. Magnificent chandeliers spectacularize main receiving areas. And
a panoramic view of Miami and Biscayne Bay makes a breathtaking
impact on us as we enter and we're greeted by a beaming Tova. Though
perhaps a pound or two heavier, she is still radiant and beautiful.

We still hadn't gotten over this heavenly abode, when she tells us of
Erwin's equally grandiose digs in Sao Paulo, Zurich and Manhattan.
Next to the splendor of his residence, Erwin stands in simple contrast.
He is a short, humble, kindly gentleman. Two years ago he had lost his
beautiful wife, Madeleine, and now he sees Tova --not as a *replace-*
ment, but as he puts it, *a continuation.* We love the way he turns to her
and says: *Tova! You've got me. And you've got me good!* They hold

hands sweetly during dinner and a few inches from the Auschwitz ID number tatooed on his forearm he wears a gold bracelet matching the one on Tova's right wrist. The bracelets can only be removed with a special screwdriver. *And I threw it away,* he said.

We talk about our firm doing public relations work for his newest company, Herling Applied Technologies, Ltd. He has patented a process that transforms phosphor gypsum, a potentially toxic waste material, into a marvelously, adaptable new building material. It could even be converted into an elastic paint that expands and contracts with metal and even absorbs alpha radiation. *If it had been painted with this material, Chernobyl wouldn't have happened,* said Frank Keenan, one of Erwin's closest associates. And it could coat ordinary trash and make it into a natural covering for wires, that would extend the recycling process to all types of waste material. *Not a substitute for recycling, but a continuation,* I thought. I offered to introduce him to Pablo Hoffman at First Equity Lenders, a Miami underwriter who could take such a hot new product immediately to the public. Meanwhile, Tova asked if we could do a little publicity for a party she was giving at the Alexander, sort of a coming out party for her and Erwin. *Sure,* I said. *Anything for you, Tova.* We got a nice photo of her and Erwin published in *Palm Beach Society Magazine* and Thom Smith did a column in the *Palm Beach Post* on the 40-plus carat sapphire ring Erwin had given her on their engagement. The ring once belonged to the Duchess of Windsor.

Twirling With Herling

I really don't know why I gravitate so strongly to Jewish people and vice versa, not to mention pastrami on rye bread and matzo ball soup. Could it be because I was born on Yom Kippur? Was it an accident that my three closest, lifelong friends, Bill Schulkin, Glenn Kray and Larry Linderman, with whom I graduated from Temple University, are Jewish? Does it have something to do with my father's first wife being Jewish or that my half brothers, Jay Madden, an engineer, and Donald Madden, a cartoonist with *Playboy* for many years, have a Jewish mother? Or could it be the way my dad, an Irishman, played Kol Nidre on his violin so powerfully? Or why Rabbi Bernie Mandelbaum used to call me one of *The Righteous* for helping him to promote his scholarships for Jewish studies given in living memory in the name of a Jewish child murdered in the Holocaust? Can any of this explain why my wife and I are so drawn to Erwin and Tova?

Until we visited them in Erwin's Fifth Avenue apartment overlooking the ice skating rink that Donald Trump expanded in Central Park, we couldn't imagine anything topping his Miami Beach penthouse. But Erwin's Manhattan residence was beyond an apartment. It was more like a private wing of The Metropolitan Museum of Art. In one room were original Renoirs, a VanGogh, a Chagall and an exquisitely soft and delicate Monet. In another room was an original Toulouse-Latrec, a Gainsborough and masterpieces continued along a corridor leading to bedrooms and sitting rooms . . . so many paintings, so many rooms that I lost count, not to mention my way back to his living room where Erwin was showing Angela a coin that had his head engraved on it in solid gold. It had been minted by a grateful Eastern European government. When we asked if he preferred being introduced as Dr. or Mr. Herling, he said he would love to answer to *Handsome Herling.*

Twirling is how one collects forkfuls of spaghetti against a spoon, converting them into more manageable mouthfuls. It's also how a Spin Man ties some loose ends, like a Broadway producer who owes him money. I thought of a way Erwin might help me to get Mark Schwartz to fork over payment for services rendered, since neither correspondence, nor phone calls from my attorney were having much of an impact. Then a funny thing happened on the way to the forum I'm envisioning for Schwartz. One of Erwin's favorite films turns out to be *The Producers* with Zero Mostel, who plays a schlock producer who sells investors more than one hundred percent of his Broadway musicals, including *Springtime For Hitler.* Since investors don't ask for such an accounting when a show closes fast, Mostel makes more money on flops. He pockets the difference between what was spent on the production and what was raised from backers. Before I could even propose my plan, Erwin sees the picture and beats me to it. He offers to help me get even with Schwartz. *We'll invite him here to my apartment. He will look at the art. We will tell him we want to invest in his shows, but we don't make a move unless we go through our friend, Tom Madden.*

Reader, by now this masterful plot should have hatched and hopefully I'll be divulging the happy outcome on Oprah. So please stay tuned! Erwin, Tova and I may win a Tony for this.

Dr. Rath Goes to Washington

Dr. Rath, there you go again. He puts out a news release under the headline "Top Scientist Invited to Inauguration of President Clinton." It carefully omits the phrase *along with everybody else in the country* and injects instead this choice bit of Rathian hyperbole:

> "This invitation is no coincidence. The highest levels of government in the most powerful nation now understand that mankind can liberate itself from the yoke of the cardiovascular epidemic."

The release proclaims the 21st Century: "The Century of Eradicating Heart Disease." I wish it also could be the century of eradicating hype.

Still Schtupin?

As a result of our PR efforts on behalf of Physicians Health & Diagnostics, a nurse pushes a 95-year-old Jewish man sitting in a wheelchair into one of our client's impotency treatment centers. He asks: So vutz the next step? Ve'er inna hurry!"

A Casualty Of The Vodka Wars?

Frank Pesce's Russian partner and friend, Vladmir Jamnikov, never fully recovered from the mysterious beating he had received shortly before he was to testify at the trial against PepsiCo. And he never got to savor the victory of seeing Cristall Vodka reappear in stores across America—finally divorced from *Stolichnaya*—and now distributed by McCormick. Or the great story we got in *FORTUNE*. For in January 1997, Jamnikov died from kidney failure.

Foggy Airport Scene: Take Two

I never heard back from Denese Tepperman. She finally must have gotten her exit visa from Fred. And someone else must have taken her to the plane. And though she may be gone from my life . . . I'll always have Newark. And I have my spin job to do. And where I spin, she can't follow. What I've got to do, she can't be any part of. Now I'm no good at being noble, but it doesn't take much to see that the problems of two little people don't amount to a hill of beans in this crazy world.

The Thighs Have It

Some publicists will go all out for a media placement. Like our Margie! Her thighs are scheduled to appear in a story she places in an April 1997 issue of *Woman's World* about liposuction. It will describe in vivid *before* and *after* pictures what a wonderful job our client Dr. Hernandez did in slimming her down. Dr. Hernandez is ecstatic.

Dinner With Regis

I'm thinking of how to wrap up this book when an idea for an ending occurs to me over dinner with Regis Philbin the other night. We're at Fulvio's, a cute little family-run Italian restaurant in Davie, Florida. Regis is between shows at nearby Bailey Hall. He's eating all the fried mozzarella sticks and inquiring what vitamins were good for his heart. My wife, as usual, is being charming, witty and energetic and tossing out ideas for bits he might do on *Regis and Kathy Lee* like hiring himself out as a babysitter. *Hear that Gelman?* Regis calls to his producer across the table. Meanwhile, she tactfully avoids mentioning something that once ticked Regis off back in New York years ago.

I was in Los Angeles at the time and my wife was handling publicity for an event at The Plaza sponsored by Metropolitan Life. Met Life had brought in Bob Hope to entertain and our mission that night was to see that when media interviewed Hope, they'd also interview Met Life's then chairman, John Creedon. And who walks into the cocktail hour but Regis with a camera crew. Angela runs over and offers assistance.

"Where's Bob Hope?" Regis asks.

"I'll get him, but please could you also interview Met Life's chairman with Mr. Hope?"

"No I just want Bob Hope."

"But really, couldn't you also just ask Mr. Creedon a question?"

"Look, I'm just here for Bob Hope. Get me Bob Hope."

"But Tom Madden would appreciate if you could interview both of them."

"Who is Tom Madden?"

(Pause) "He's my husband. He was Vice President of NBC. He's in California tonight."

"All right. All right. Get the two of them."

Belatedly, I wish to thank Regis for interviewing our client that night. And I'd like to thank all of the talk show hosts, producers, directors, reporters, writers, interviewers, photographers, editors, sound engineers, lighting technicians, camera operators and talent coordinators for helping us to serve our clients. And especially to our clients, I'd like to say as Bob Hope always says . . . **Thanks for the memories!**

Alas, This Dagger

At the last minute *Woman's World* pulls the liposuction article scheduled to appear in the April issue that was going to include Margie's thighs. They decide to focus on a particular technique, which our plastic surgeon client doesn't use because it's too new and might cause complications. So now we go from being ecstatic to crushed. That's the PR business for you. Sometimes it's heaven. Other times it's a root canal.

Ooops

Whatever I said about Harvey Tauman, I take it all back. . . . . . .we just got rehired by Hydron.

DREAM or NIGHTMARE?

The musical *DREAM* opened April 3, 1997, on Broadway at the Royale Theatre. In his review in *The New York Times,* Peter Marks described it as "a grab-bag variety show" and "as retro as revisiting one of those kaleidoscopic numbers by the June Taylor Dancers." He said that "for nostalgic buffs and lovers of Mercer's lyrics, smooth as polished marble, 'Dream' may be a godsend, an animated jukebox of burnished melodies. But for virtually everyone else the revue may seem pretty lame."

Oh, remember Carl DeSantis? He hit it big . . . wound up selling Rexall Sundown for $1.8 billion. He credits our publicity with helping the company he founded become the world's leading nutritional supplement company. To this day, Carl is still a TransMedia Group client and his next big winner just might be a calorie-burning beverage called Celsius. You read it here!

CURTAIN

Epilogue

Sic'em Tiger Bugs!

Let's return one last time to our reception room so I can show you some losers I wish we never had as clients as they either wasted our time or cost us money. Let's start with a giant toothpick for dinner. The scrappy, theatrical-looking man sitting with the jar on his lap is Richard C. Fox, CEO of Microterra. Inside the jar are millions of LSU Tiger Bugs trained to be voracious eaters of toxic chemicals impregnated in telephone poles. Fox thinks there's money in recycling telephone poles and he wants to sic his microbes on old poles to rid them of chemicals so they can be safely disposed of or recycled into other products. Microterra runs up a tab with our firm and then merges with a company in California, which in turn changes it's name and the trail gets so confusing our attorney tells us to forget the debt because it's too complicated and would be too costly to collect. How do you sue a microbe anyway? Even if you win, they'll never pay you.

Mummy Dearest

And I suppose you're wondering what's in the long box across the lap of the grim-looking chap to the left of Mr. Fox. It's a pre-Ptolemaic sarcophagus circa 367-284 B.C. It contains a group of Egyptian mummies consisting of a child, estimated to be nine or ten at the time of demise and three mummified pets, a rodent, a lion and a lizard. Yes, we get all kinds in Boca Raton. Anyway, the owner, Alexander Schwerter, wants us to publicize his mummies as he has just heard that pop superstar Michael Jackson just paid 3 million for an Egyptian Mummy, a young prince who died 2,400 years ago, in the belief it will help him to achieve the immortality he craves.

Vivante!

The two amiable fellows are Mishka Jett and Peter Newton who started a company called Vivante Pharmaceuticals, which took off like a rocket, but came crashing back to earth when news reports surfaced that Mishka, in a previous life, had pled no contest to a charge that he had misused funds that were entrusted to him. Somehow this was not disclosed in their recent public offering. And now they've wasted about 15 hours of our time billing and cooing over new packaging designs we created for them on spec for their line of never-to-be skin care products. And as Mishka and Peter run from irate investors, guess who's still holding a bag full of packaging ideas? Finally, that chubby chap is Leslie Greyling of South Africa, who wanted to be a client of ours. Thank God we declined as he too has a posse of investors and creditors after him and eventually he wound up in the hoosegow.

EXT. BUILDING AND LOAN OFFICES -- NIGHT
PAN SHOT -- As George runs by:

GEORGE
Merry Christmas, you wonderful old Building and Loan!

–It's A Wonderful Life

I can't end this book without telling you about a new account we're getting, a new type of mortgage banker. I'm so excited about this new client. It's a company going on the American Stock Exchange called Amquest. But we haven't received the check yet. Not that there's a problem. We had a great first meeting. But we don't start working until we get the check. We've been burned, which is why I exhort our account executives not to be bashful about asking for payment. I'm always preaching: *Don't let clients fall behind in their monthly fees.* Our staff dislikes asking for money, but I tell them it's not a good idea to separate service and payment. How else are we going to meet the payroll? All right, I'll say it: *Show me the money!*

David Morgenstern looks like he could play Clark Kent in a *Superman* movie. He's a preppy-looking guy you'd guess to be in his thirties, but he's 48. He wears glasses and looks trim in a well-tailored, neatly coordinated suit and tie. His hair is cut short. He has a handsome, clean-shaven square face. Overall, he makes a crisp, if not a snappy, appearance. While he's cordial, he seems shy, yet there's an aura of energy about him, maybe a vestige of his earlier days in the coal mining, oil and gas business in Tennessee. And he has what I believe is one helluva great idea—a whole new concept in mortgage lending. And I know I can publicize the hell out of it.

We're planning to promote his idea as a return to the good ole days of the Bailey Building & Loan. I want to rekindle those homey images of a bygone era when the hometown lender really cared about its customers . . . about how they were making out . . . getting along in their lives. In those more personal days, nobody was just an anonymous borrower like today. Bailey's customers were people. Neighbors. Friends. And the warm-hearted Building & Loan had a deep, abiding interest in their lives. It was indeed a wonderful life.

Morgenstern has developed a program aimed at the 70 million, mid-level home buyers in the U.S. who are so preoccupied with making their loan payment that they're shut out of investing in their future. Morgenstern plans to change all that. He's going to build into loan payments an investment in equities like value funds and life insurance. It will be a combined payment that will make borrowers also equity investors. And it will solve a common problem of people trying to figure out a maze of investment options that's so perplexing and baffling today that it paralyzes people from investing. *It will be built into our product so they don't have to figure out where to invest their money.* They'll be putting savings into mutual funds designed to preserve their capital.

I'm excited to hear it because it's new, which is where the word *news* comes from. And in *news releases* we'll spread that news. I'm even thinking we'll give bags of bread and salt to borrowers just like Jimmy Stewart did in *It's A Wonderful Life.* When I ask Morgenstern to tell me a little about himself, I'm stunned by his matter-of-fact reply.

"I'm a convicted felon. I've served time in a Federal prison." He says it calmly, automatically, like someone telling you they're a recovering alcoholic.

"And it's the best thing that ever happened to me."
"How's that?" I asked fascinated.
"I found Jesus Christ."

He related the whole grisly story as if recounting a bad dream. Only it was true. And it's all disclosed in his company's 10Q and other public filings. He wasn't hiding anything. He had made mistakes. Serious ones. Got caught up in a financial helter skelter. Committed bank fraud. Was convicted. Sentenced. It was a long time ago. Fifteen years ago.

He had made a fortune in the energy business. Had a net worth of $30 million. A happy marriage. A beautiful home. Then after President Reagan was elected the bottom fell out. The savings and loan crisis erupted. Institutions tried camouflaging bad investments, whose value was eroding faster than loans could prop them up. Morgenstern said he and his bank conspired to falsify documents that would make his business look better than it was. But it was losing money. And he was getting deeper and deeper into the scheme until the Feds swarmed in. He lost everything. His business ruined. Personal wealth gone. Disgraced. His marriage ended in divorce. And off he went to prison . . . to discover the Lord.

When he was released after serving nearly 19 months . . . *My life shifted.* Today he is remarried to his wife. They have five children, ranging in ages from 1 to 14. He's a deacon at Calvary Chapel Church in Fort Lauderdale. Teaches bible studies class. He's a scoutmaster. And an honest businessman who has felt the frustration of having to start over . . . of having to pay off a mortgage with little left over with which to invest and start building a future. And that's what his program is designed to change. He has created his own portfolio of value mutual funds, has obtained the necessary approvals from regulators, and is about to launch his collateralized mortgage investment program. And he has signed a letter of agreement to acquire one of the country's premier flagship residential realty companies, which hasn't yet been consolidated into a conglomerate.

I can't wait to start working for this man who's been saved . . . who has turned his life around and now wants to turn many lives around. For redemption is the greatest story one could tell. So I expect this spin will be uplifting.

The Spin of Tobacco

Thus it came to pass that there went out a moral decree from Caesar Attorneys General that a heavy fine shall be levied against Big Tobacco for its transgressions against the people.

Another inexplicably hot summer rolls over us. Local TV meteorologists are at it again—hosting endless programs on hurricane preparedness, putting their own spin on the big spins a comin'. They seem brought to us every year by hurricane shutter companies who won't rest until we're all rolled up like sardines in tins. But the big news every day is not about storms, however. It concerns our state's case against Big Tobacco. Last week Florida lost a legal skirmish, but the higher court left the main part of its mega lawsuit intact. Big Tobacco put its spin on the development. Anti-tobacco forces put theirs. Yet the war's outcome seems inevitable now. Through the smoke, *We The People* were beginning to see victory ahead.

Now great moral issues have a way of washing up like seaweed on your private beach. Today it washed up on ours like a beached whale and set off so many contradictory thoughts that it made my head spin.

I had just come out of the surf after a cool, refreshing swim off Manalapan Beach. The last thing on my mind was a pack of cigarettes. But what do I see gleaming white in the sand before me — an unopened pack of *Merit Ultra Lights*. The orphan wrapped in cellophane had washed ashore, despoiling our pristine beach. Upon closer inspection, however, it was Martian dry and fresh as if it had just popped out of a vending machine.

Like Hamlet over Yorick, I stood over the intruder wondering where it came from, then picked it up and looked up and down the beach for whomever might have dropped it. About a hundred yards to the north were four women, including two adults and two teenagers moping alone the water's edge. The adults looked like they might be the girls' mothers. It must have been one of them who dropped it, so I started after them. But then thorny moral issues began to pinch me like broken shells as I jogged towards them.

Was I about to help someone to continue to commit suicide? Was I some kind of Dr. Kevorkian in a bathing suit? My impulse was to stop and throw the pack away. But would I be helping Big Tobacco to sell another pack of its lethal products? Surely the person who lost it would straightaway buy another. What if one of the youngsters had dropped it? What if she had been concealing her habit from her parents? Would I be one of those do-gooders who get people into trouble because of their self-righteous nosiness? On the other hand, maybe I <u>should</u> turn her in. The sneak!

As I got closer, I noticed one of the women was incredibly skinny. She looked as if she had been rescued from a concentration-camp. Could this be the smoker? Would I be returning her to her poison gas chamber? Hell with it. I'll throw the damn pack away! But would that be stealing? Destroying someone's property? Did I have the right? Okay, I'll take it home. Sure, then everyone will think I'm a hypocrite for not allowing people to smoke in our apartment.

I can't bear this infernal dilemma anymore. I start to run. I just want to get rid of it. Wash my hands like Pontius Pilate. Return it to the rightful idiot who carelessly dropped it. So what if people smoke? It's their life. There are no "no smoking" sections outdoors. I thought of Philip Morris and its motto, *Veni Vedi Vici*. Why was this their motto? Why not *E Pluribus Unum* or *habeas corpus*?

Now here I was...running along the beach carrying the *corpus delicti* in my hand as if it were a twisted baton and I'm in some perverted relay race. Was this insane? Look at the moral choices?

Keep it? I'm a hypocrite. Throw it away? I'm a thief and litterbug. Give it to that poor, emaciated girl? I'm a Nazi. Hand it over to the teenager? I'm corrupting her. Or I'm a squealer and a rat. Give it back to one of the chain-smoking adults? I'm Dr. Kevorkian. Nearly out of breath, I catch up with them.

Did one of you drop this? I pant. *No,* they said, looking at me as if I'm some kind of nut.

Then I spot another walker about 50 yards ahead. I start running to her. This was ridiculous. I had become addicted to returning cigarettes. I couldn't stop.

Are these yours? I asked the lone walker, gasping. It was as if I had asked if she sucked turtle eggs. *No,* she declared.

So what do I do? Do I keep them until a doctor ever gives me a month to live, then smoke them? Then there came a brilliant light. An ultra bright idea. I'll return this unopened pack of cigarettes to a store and get someone's money back, then send it to The American Cancer Society. "Oh just put them away," my wife said. "Why do you have to make such a big deal?"

THE END

Appendix I

Why do I need public relations?

Why indeed public relations? Shouldn't I put more money into advertising? Why should I take away from other budgets when public relations can't guarantee me a single exposure?

These are questions I've been asked over and over. And I've built a successful PR business answering them. Our firm has helped clients, from small businesses to some of America's largest corporations, to better understand the value of public relations. At first, some were skeptical. When they saw how it could increase sales or the price of their stock, they became believers.

The answer is simple. Public relations is like a stealth bomber over a targeted market. Its messages are factual. Persuasive! They penetrate consumers' defenses against the advertising onslaught. Who can resist an editorial invasion? PR deals with the stuff that credibility is made of. Delivered by media, its messages bear the trappings of third-party endorsement. And because they aren't bought and paid for like ads, they are more believable. More valuable. If not priceless. No wonder public relations is so highly effective at building consensus. At creating consent. At winning new business friendships in the form of customer loyalty, investor approval and community respect.

No business today can flourish without such a key component in its marketing arsenal. It starts with choosing a rifle over a club.

Eventually it becomes the a la mode on the marketing pie. Sometimes it's the spice in the recipe. More often, it's the ingredient producing the most impressive results.

While advertising can channel awareness into action, public relations is the sweeter salvo with its subtle power to create that awareness in the first place, to overcome barriers and make other marketing efforts more effective. It can ameliorate deep-seated bias or combat a crisis. And remove a blotch from an organization's chart with a surgeon's skill.

For these reasons, public relations should be an integral part, if not the main part, of the marketing program of any modern business enterprise.

Appendix II

**WOULD TALKING TO 50 MILLION TV VIEWERS MAKE YOU NERVOUS?
IT SHOULDN'T, IF YOU FOLLOW THESE TIPS.**

Few public relations firms have prepared as many executives to appear on television as we have. Here are our tips on how to maximize your effectiveness on camera:

- Don't overly rehearse. Unless you're a great actor, chances are you'll come across sounding studied and stiff.

- Wear comfortable clothes that fit your concept. If you're representing a sporting goods company, you'll look much more natural in a casual golf shirt than in a suit and tie.

- Forget the camera. Talk to the person asking you questions. If you concentrate on the interviewer, you'll forget all the technical stuff going on around you.

- Be friendly. All those disarming qualities that go into making a good first impression in business are even more important on television, like enthusiasm, politeness and maybe once in a while a smile.

- Sit up straight. No slouching, rocking, squirming, swiveling or lint picking. The television screen tends to exaggerate extraneous movement.

- Be concise. You'll be amazed how quickly the time goes by. Limit your main points to just a few, and keep your remarks brief.

- If you're nervous, so what! Use the energy positively. Anyone who doesn't feel at least a little tense about appearing on camera should have their blood pressure checked. Odds are that only you will know you're shaking.

- Don't stand up and shake hands until the director tells you it's over. Until the tape is checked back in the control room, the interview isn't over. Wait until you hear from the floor director and someone removes your microphone.

- Be patient. You're in good hands. The camera crew, the director, everyone on the set are doing their best to make you look good. They're on your side.

- Keep in mind that television is a visual media. What viewers see is probably more important than what they hear. Through your publicist, offer some visual materials such as background video (called B-Roll), photographs, slides, charts, etc.

- If you're lucky enough to have a professional publicist representing you, let the professional handle all of the booking arrangements.

Appendix III

Here are clients I've had over the years who—for one reason or another—have earned a permanent position on . . .

THE ALL-MADDEN PR CLIENT TEAM

AT&T
Barclay International Realty
Ben's Best Kosher Deli
Biosonics
Boca Raton Museum of Art
City of New York
Coit Carpet and Drapery Cleaning
Commercial Science, Inc.
Communication Service Centers
Compass Health Systems
Consumer Savings Centers (C$C)
Drexel Burnham Lambert Real Estate
Douglas R. Stringham M.D.
Eduard Nakhamkin Fine Arts
Elke Sommer
Frank Pesce Group
Gunster Yoakley, Valdes-Fauli & Stewart, P.A.

Global Horizons
Hydron Technologies
Imaging Diagnostic Systems
International Health Products
Jackson Memorial Foundation
Kathryn Crosby
Leonardo Patterson
Melanie Taylor Kent
Metropolitan Life
National Arthritis Foundation
National Italian American Foundation
Navarro Security
Ney Piniero
Physicians Health & Diagnostics
Princess Yasmin Aga Khan
Rexall Sundown, Inc.
Strang-Cornell Medical Center
Vivian Hernandez M.D.

Index

THOMAS MADDEN is chairman and CEO of TransMedia Public Relations, one of the largest public relations and marketing firms in the Southeast.

Madden began his career as a journalist, working as a reporter for *The Philadelphia Inquirer*. He decided to switch careers after getting punched out cold while on assignment and landed a job with ABC, where he worked as director of public relations. He jumped over to NBC to accept the position of vice president and assistant to then-president, Fred Silverman.

In 1981, Madden struck out on his own. He and his wife, Angela, co-founded TransMedia in New York City. Seven years later, they moved the award-winning firm to Boca Raton, Florida. Madden's success has earned him coverage in *Time Magazine*, *The Wall Street Journal*, *Forbes*, and *The New York Times*.

TransMedia's clients have included AT&T, Drexel Burnham Lambert, the City of New York, Mayor Koch, and Rexall Sundown. The firm also regularly books corporate spokespersons, authors, medical experts, entrepreneurs and celebrities on network and nationally-syndicated radio and television programs.

If you would like to contact the author,
you may write to him in care of:

TransMedia Group
240 W. Palmetto Park Rd., Suite 300
Boca Raton, FL 33432
P (561) 750–9800
F (561) 750–4660
www.transmediagroup.com